THE
PURI

THE ORIGINS AND PURPOSE OF LIFE

GENESIS 1 TO 11 / NEVILLE CARR

AN ALBATROSS BOOK

 the bible reading fellowship
OPENING THE BIBLE

© Commentary: Neville Carr 1992
© Discussion questions: Albatross Books Pty Ltd 1992

Published in Australia and New Zealand by
Albatross Books Pty Ltd
PO Box 320, Sutherland
NSW 2232, Australia
in the United States of America by
Albatross Books
PO Box 131, Claremont
CA 91711, USA
and in the United Kingdom by
The Bible Reading Fellowship
Peter's Way, Sandy Lane West
Oxford OX4 5HG, England

First edition 1992
Reprinted 1993

National Library of Australia
Cataloguing-in-Publication data

Carr, Neville
The Origins and Purpose of Life

ISBN 0 86760 142 6 (Albatross)
ISBN 0 7459 2190 6 (BRF)

1. Bible. O.T. Genesis I–XI — Commentaries.
I. Title

222.1107

Cover photo: John Waterhouse
Printed and bound in Australia by McPherson's Printing Group, Victoria

Contents

Foreword

My understanding of biblical Christianity has benefited enormously from the many insights of various teachers and scholars: Moore College staff while I was a student there, Barbara Thiering of Sydney University, J.A. Thompson and Adam Murtonen of Melbourne University; and, over the past twenty years, the seminal thinking and personal encouragement of Robert Banks.

Having taught Genesis 1 to 11 in different settings, I'm certain about its importance for a proper understanding of 'the whole purpose of God'. A more succinct and profound statement about the meaning of life would be hard to find in literature, art, music or other media. Along with Isaiah 40 to 66 and Ecclesiastes, it is for me a favourite part of the Old Testament.

I take full responsibility for the limitations of this material and acknowledge that many ideas contained in it are not original. The aim of this book is to suggest ways of interpreting Genesis 1 to 11 that make direct connections with contemporary society and culture, while at the same time provoking thinking people to look carefully at the primitive biblical account of the origin, purpose and characteristics of life in God's world.

My own spiritual and intellectual pilgrimage has been empowered by the strength and security of God's faithfulness and by the love, tolerance and encouragement of family and friends. I therefore dedicate this book to my parents, Connie and Gordon, my sister and brother-in-law, Isabel and Don, and my wife and mentor, Elspeth.

Neville Carr
May 1992

Introduction

MOST TALKS I HEAR ON the Old Testament are remote from the culture and society I belong to and struggle to understand. This book aims to show how one small but seminal part of the Old Testament provides us with vital clues for dealing critically and constructively with the social and material forces which shape us all.

My desire in writing this book is, first, to provide preachers, small group leaders and educators with a resource to rediscover the central place of these chapters of Genesis in understanding the Bible; and, second, to provide inquirers into religion with a glimpse of how useful and relevant they are for living in a complex, confusing and often dehumanising society.

From these chapters of Genesis, the early Israelites found strength and understanding in such times of national crisis as threats of annihilation by Egyptians,

Philistines, Assyrians and Babylonians, and in such cases of individual suffering as those recorded in Psalms and Job. In our times of difficulty, I believe we can do the same.

What can we find in this book that will provide us with the best framework for our lives?

* **First**, *God the creator is in charge of the world*. This conviction plays a pivotal role when the forces of chaos and death threaten to overwhelm us through the political and economic systems of the day. God, we see in these chapters, is in charge of his world, despite appearances to the contrary, and will never relinquish his purpose to bless it and achieve his will through it.

* **Second**, *women and men, caring partners in creation, have significance*. When women across the world are increasingly marginalised and oppressed by men who justify such behaviour in the name of religion, biology, psychology or history, it is timely for us to look again at the original blueprint, here in Genesis, for the way in which the sexes were called into a partnership of equals, to care for creation and properly manage its resources. This provides the basis of human dignity. Such a basis can resist the inroads of an increasingly technological society.

* **Third,** *there is a clear answer to the purpose of our existence.* We are told that our task is to replenish, order, name and cultivate the created world. Many believe this is God's affirmation of the cultural, scientific and ecological enterprises we engage in today.

* **Fourth,** *marriage, sexuality and community are blessed by God.* Contemporary trends in sexuality are of community concern, with the problem of AIDS and the practice of biotechnology and genetic engineering. The picture of community in these early chapters of Genesis has something of value to say to us, even though our circumstances are different.

* **Fifth,** *the problem of evil is central.* It reveals itself in the flawedness of human wisdom and in self-interest. Given that God made us all with a capacity for choosing to live inside or outside his boundaries, Genesis 3 to 11 maps the consequences of the choice to erect alternative ground rules.

* **Sixth,** *individual decisions affect the whole of society.* For those who have imbibed the popular piety of individualism, this section provides a salutary reminder that every human action has its social ramifications — that there

is a solidarity between us, our circle of relationships and the kind of world our choices produce.

∗ **Seventh**, *once we turn our back on God, our attempt to regain control of the chaos raises problems.* Humans have always sought to regain control of the chaos resulting from their fundamental decision to ignore God and his ways. Two modern methods of doing this are through faith in a social order divorced from God — our secularised society — and our tendency to be dominated by technology.

Throughout these chapters we will see how these principles not only affect Israelite society, but our own as well.

Discussion questions

Talking it through

1 The book of Genesis was written for the people of Israel as they experienced national disintegration and exile in Babylon. What would have been the book's special appeal to a harassed people? How would they have gained strength from the early chapters of Genesis?

2 Think about the twin concepts of exploiting and caring for the environment. Do they have to be in conflict?

3 Why is everything we do flawed? Is technology able to overcome some of the inherent chaos?

4 Think about the ability of modern science to grow an embryo in a test tube, or to fertilise a surrogate mother. Does marriage still have a place in this new world created by science? Why?

Widening our horizons

1 Think of the world in which we live, with its wars, famines and natural catastrophes. How do you reconcile this disturbing reality with the apparently absurd idea that God is still in charge?

2 Is there a single, cohesive, *central* reason for our existence? Provide answers that might be given by each of the following:
(a) the successful business person whose life goals are restricted to the material world
(b) the young woman who has just married the man of her dreams
(c) the young mother, poorly educated and with limited social skills, in the outer suburbs
(d) a Christian paraplegic or community worker.
What reason for living most satisfies you?

3 'I can do this. It doesn't affect anybody else.' True or false? How do individual decisions affect relationships?

4 Society's domination by technology is an
attempt to restore order out of chaos. Why
has technology not solved immoral behaviour
in the following areas:

(a) financial fraud (banking, tax evasion,
    insider trading on the stock exchange)?

(b) corporate crime (computer fraud,
    organised theft of private vehicles)?

(c) vandalism (theft of private property,
    malicious damage to public property)?

(d) gambling (casinos, the TAB, SP
    bookmaking, club poker machines)?

Do we solve these problems by putting
new labels on them: 'antisocial behaviour',
'victimless crime', 'the product of a disturbed
personality', 'a harmless fling'? Are these
labels true or the whole story?

1
Order out of chaos

Why read the story of creation?
GENESIS CHAPTER 1, VERSE 1 TO
CHAPTER 2, VERSE 4A

A SURVEY OF CHURCHGOERS has shown that a majority of Baptists and Pentecostals believe the world is more evil than good; minorities in a number of other churches agree.[1] When we are confronted day and night through the media by the signs of social chaos, family breakdown, racial tension, international violence and the polarities between rich and poor, it is understandable that some Christians take a pessimistic world view.

This conviction often leads to withdrawal from a world which is 'evil', and to an irrelevance within the culture and technology of change.

Whatever forces of chaos and destructiveness sur-

rounded the audience which the writer of Genesis
1 to11 was addressing, the message of comfort and
hope was designed to lift the sights of the audience
from its own oppression or apparent hopelessness[2]
to God's purposes for his creation.

The purpose of the creation stories

The primary purpose of the creation stories was
not to explain the *origins* of the world and of
humanity, but to answer concerns about the
stability and orderliness of the world.[3] Ludwig Kohler
says the creation story answers the question, 'What
gives Israelite history its significance?' with the
reply, 'God has given to the history of the people
of God its meaning by the creation.'[4] For the writer
of Genesis 1, the bottom line is God's supremacy
as creator. It is this that gives ultimate security in
such times of national turbulance as the time of
exile.

The God who rescued Israel from Egypt — lead-
ing the nation into the land promised to Abraham
and the patriarchs and guiding their future via the
code of ethics given on Mount Sinai — was the God
who brought order out of primeval chaos and who
provided the necessary resources for his creatures to
live well in fellowship with himself. If, as is likely,
Genesis 1 to 11 was edited finally at the time before
Israel's return from exile, then it comes as a message
of hope.[5]

God is in charge (chapter 1, verses 1 and 2)

However we translate the opening lines in Genesis 1, the fundamental point is a reassuring one: that God is responsible for the creation of the whole universe. The vehicle of creation is the divine word: 'And God said, "Let there be. . ."' God created the darkness and the light, but separated darkness from the light and called the light 'good'.

There is an inequality from the very beginning: it is light alone which receives God's approval. Darkness and evil have always been linked together; in the Old Testament, they have often been linked to death and the land of non-being.[6]

The message of hope is that God overpowers or wards off the threat of darkness through his creative word or act. His word transforms the darkness. Whatever little we know about God at this stage, it is clear that he is in charge, that his command is effective. What he commands *happens*. However short our history is as creatures, his life goes back into the ages. He is the author of time itself.

The 'good news' for today's reader of these opening chapters of the Old Testament is that God the creator is the one 'in the beginning' who established order and called his creatures to continue the process in a world where chaos and darkness are threatening. Which ever translation one prefers of these first three verses,[7] the thrust seems to be clear: When God began to create the heaven and earth, he disrupted and transformed the disorder and darkness by means of a decision expressed through a word. The reader is not told about the audience to which the divine utterance is directed, nor by what means the writer could have sensed God's preference for light.

The phrase *ruah elohim* is often translated 'Spirit of God' or 'mighty wind' (verse 2), as if God's way of acting on creation was through the chaotic storm. The picture of a storm 'hovering' over the waters suggests that God restrains the watery chaos through his breath.[8]

Through his breath, wind or voice, Yahweh — a Hebrew name for God — established supremacy over 'the chief threat to his sovereignty, the insurgent sea'.[9] There is no suggestion of an *ex nihilo* ('from nothing') creation. Creation has more to do with *dividing and ordering* — light-darkness, waters beneath-above the firmament, heaven-earth, day-night, sun-moon. It is the 'bringing of order out of chaos, meaning out of meaninglessness, form out of the formless'.[10]

The cosmos pre-exists, needing only to be, as Robert Luyster says, 'revealed, organised and defended against further reductions to a chaotic state'.[11] The suggestion is of a 'creation that urgently needs to be disciplined' and of a God 'who goes on curbing forces that threaten the life of the world'.[12] As in the Babylonian creation epic, *Enuma Elish*,[13] the act of creation involves a reforming of pre-existent threatening forces, through the instrumentality of a divine word acting through agents such as sun, moon, waters and wind. This is the force of the sentence, 'The earth having been formless and void'. The noun *tohu* denotes a 'trackless, howling wilderness' and thus represents emptiness.[14]

This chapter needs to be studied more in terms of what it reveals about God the creator and his purposes for creation and less in terms of how or when he made things. It seems fruitless to get sidetracked by questions like, 'Was a day intended as a twenty-four hour period?' It is the only concept the author had for time, unlike our scientific age with its fine gradations. He is more concerned with painting a global picture of creation than with listing with scientific precision all the details and chronology of the creation process. The central truth of this chapter is in the first verse: 'In the beginning God'. The rest is a description of how God went about his work and of its impact thereafter.

How God went about the work of creation (chapter 1, verses 3 to 30)

❏ *Whatever God said, happened*

Perhaps the contrast for the writer was between the pronouncements of pagan rulers or Israel's false prophets, and actualities (see Ezekiel 12, verses 25 and 28; and Ezekiel 13, verses 6 and 7).

God's integrity is measured by the match between his word, an expression of his thoughts, and his action (see Isaiah 55, verse 11). Our faith in him is based on the trustworthiness of his word. When he speaks, what he says happens. Many words uttered today, as in the past, are empty words, because their basis of authority is not divine, but flawed human wisdom.

The fourth work of creation (verses 11 to 13) takes a different form, in that the word no longer activates the deed directly, but what has already been created, the earth, becomes the source of further creative activity within itself. The creativity involves a division of all plants according to their kind. Claus Westermann says, 'By the command of the creator, vegetation is a subdivided whole, not an unorganised mass.'[15] However, it is once again God's creative word-action that empowers the vegetation to be fruitful; it can't do so of its own accord.

❏ *God is a God of order*
The second creative day's activity consists of separating the primeval waters by means of a vault or dome (verse 6): this was thought to be a solid metallic disc whose function was to plug up the watery mass in the heavens and to regulate the flow and distribution of waters in the atmosphere, the seas and on the earth. A key idea of creation is 'separation and distinction'.[16] Like the darkness, the seas and the

watery mass are somewhat threatening, whereas the land or earth is established as the focus of all human activity.

So the creative activity of God involved the setting of boundaries. When the boundaries are transgressed, chaos returns. The flood story suggests that God could at any point reverse his original creative decision. The command, 'Let there be. . .', to be found at the beginning of each new creation activity, has a certain ambivalence or open-endedness, which somehow suggests a measure of human responsibility.

When God named each of his created works (Day, Night, Heaven, Earth, Seas), he was defining reality for all time. Boundaries had to be set by God which allowed an order or rhythm (day-night, heaven-earth, sea-land, male-female, work-rest). Daylight enables the fertilisation of plants and shrubs, and provides the time frame for normal work to take place, whereas night allows time for rest, recreation and reflection after a hard day's toil. The heavens provide the atmospheric conditions for the gases necessary to maintain and renew life in all its forms, via wind and rainfall; the earth depends for its livelihood on the regular moisture and sunlight that interact chemically with the vegetation.

❑ *God had control over the heavenly bodies*
When it comes to the creation of the heavenly bodies (verses 14 to 19), the repetition highlights the fact

that in the ancient world it was the sun (the god Shamash) and the moon that were the divinities of great importance. So the writer's intention is polemical: the sun and moon are only creatures. Their purpose consists of four functions: to divide, to indicate, to shine and to govern. They are created entities with a limited function of service that sets them apart from God or from the gods.

The lights separate day from night and determine the calendar. The fact that the names of the two main divinities are not mentioned, but referred to as greater and lesser lights indicates the desire of the writer to avoid any mythical reference.

In the ancient world the heavenly bodies were thought to stand in the centre and rule over other heavenly bodies. For the Babylonians, the luminaries foretold world events and served as one of the main forms of divine revelation. For the Hebrews, however, they served, as Brevard Childs says, as 'witnesses to the perpetuity of the creation'.[17]

This demythologising process in the biblical account, where the sun and moon are but creatures who have limited rule over day and night, reminds the people of God listening to this word that they should be critical and prophetic about the particular illusions of their society. The people of God need a similar approach to the priests and prophets of our day: meaning-givers and interpreters of modern reality such as financial analysts and economists, media moguls and purveyors of the gospel of human progress.

❏ *God means creation to be a blessing*
The creation of the water animals and birds (verses 20 to 23) signals an addition to the pattern of creation: blessing. The blessing in verse 22 speaks of procreation, fruitfulness and fertility within the animal species.

Claus Westermann reminds us that many myths occur in the ancient Near East in which creation and blessing are directly linked and 'whose effect is growth, increase and abundance'. In the primeval material, blessing is the 'power of fertility'. When the creator blesses, the blessing works itself out effectively in the life of what is blessed or of the one asking the blessing. God's blessing is most obviously visible in the gift of children.[18]

The biblical concept of blessing contains three important ideas:

* *Fertility* — fruitfulness, productivity
* *Long life* — in the New Testament, this developed into the idea of 'eternal life' or the 'life of the aeons/ages'
* *Peace* — order, harmony, balance.

Alongside these three fundamental privileges stood three parallel responsibilities:

* *Loyalty* — to God and neighbour
* *Truthfulness* — reflecting God's image and likeness
* *Justice* — commitment to a prophetic and critical role on behalf of the marginalised.

Prosperity was interpreted in the Old Testament as a sign of God's favour. It was only after the collapse of the two Israelite kingdoms and the exile in Babylon that any reflection on the role of human suffering modified this view.

Blessing in this chapter is an *unconditional* word to animals and humans, whereas the 'gospel of prosperity' commonly proclaimed today is thought to depend upon the fulfilment of religious or ethical duties.

In this earlier biblical material, there is no question of conditionality: the word of blessing is a *unilateral* decision of grace alone — it depends on the character of the promise-maker, God. The power of created life to reproduce itself is given to each species 'at its creation and therefore [is] not dependent upon subsequent rites or petitions for its effect [as in the ancient fertility cults]. . . Thus the gods are denied all power, place and function. . . whether to create, renew or rule.'[19]

❑ *God made human beings the pinnacle of creation*
For animals (verses 24 and 25), in contrast to humans, the divine blessing is absent because the

animals only indirectly receive the power of creation from God — though, according to von Rad, they receive it directly from the earth.[20] This is true of each of the three main groups: domestic, wild and small animals. The 'creeping things' are reptiles, insects and mice that keep close to the ground.[21]

God seems to be more intimately involved in the creation of humanity (verses 26 to 28) than in his earlier works, signalled by the words, 'Let us make man' (NIV).

Some have interpreted the plural 'Let us' as God addressing his heavenly court of angels; others as Christ and the Trinity; and others again as the plural of self-deliberation or of self-encouragement. Some have taken it to indicate plurality within the Godhead — especially if the word 'spirit' is retained instead of 'wind' in verse 2. Gordon Wenham says that the call to create man should be regarded as 'a divine announcement to the heavenly court, drawing the angelic host's attention to the master stroke of creation, man'.[22]

Not only is humankind seen as the pinnacle of creation by the nature of God's call; it is also signalled in terms used to describe that creation. The word *selem* ('image') in verse 26 means an actual plastic work, a duplicate, sometimes even an idol, sculpture or statue. The word *demut* which follows it in verse 26, means 'similarity', 'likeness', 'representation'. The question this raises is: what is the nature of a human being? Is a person's 'likeness-to-God' lost with the so-called 'fall' or does it remain the fundamental part of humanity?

A third indication that something more significant is happening is that the verb 'create' appears in verse 27 for the first time since the opening sentence (verse 1); in all other descriptions, the verb 'make' is used instead.

The nature and purpose of human life
❏ *Human beings are made in God's image*
As previously stated, this image has been interpreted variously as:

* humanity's reasoning and intellectual capacity;
* upright physical posture;
* ability to rule;
* bisexuality;
* potential for fellowship with God;
* humanity as God's representative on earth —
  in the same way as ancient Oriental rulers left
  busts of themselves in the provinces, as signs
  of their power and rule.[23]

Strictly speaking, *adam* does not mean the image of God, nor one who possesses the image of God, 'but only one who is like God in the manner of an image or representation'.[24] The image is perpetuated via procreation and the resources enabling humans to build community and manage God's world.

Later reflection suggested a semi-divine status that invested glory, honour and dominion over all creation (Psalm 8, verses 5 and 6; and Deuteronomy 4, verses 15 to 18). Such a view contrasted dramatically with the common image of Mesopotamian and Canaanite anthropology, which saw humans as mere servants of the gods, freeing the superior beings from more onerous duties.

The risen Christ was seen as 'the image of the invisible God', supreme in every way (Colossians 1, verses 15 to 20) and as the 'reflection of God's glory and the exact imprint of God's very being, sustaining the universe by his powerful command' (Hebrews 1, verse 3). To know the Son was to see and know the Father (John 14, verse 9).

❑ *Human beings have responsibility for the earth*
One of the major criticisms levelled at the Judaeo-Christian religion is that the command to 'subdue' or 'have dominion over' the earth (verse 28) has given free rein to environmental abuse and economic exploitation for the maximisation of profit. The focal point of these verses is the idea of responsibility for, not exploitation of the creation by humans.[25]

A fuller answer to this problem is in Genesis 2, but the first response comes from the process of creation as an ordering of chaos, a setting of boundaries and a facilitating of harmony. If chaos threatens still, humans are deputised as God's agents to ensure it doesn't return or overwhelm the creation.

In this sense, to 'subdue' or 'have dominion over' means to 'harness',[26] 'ensure harmony', 'maintain a proper balance between life-giving and life-denying forces'. Such an interpretation rules out actions which threaten the balance of the environment. There is nevertheless a clear affirmation here of scientific research and technological advancement. The historian E.H. Carr says:

> Scientists, social scientists and historians are all engaged in different branches of the same study. . . of man and his environment. . . to increase man's understanding of, and mastery over, his environment. . . The historian, like any other scientist. . . incessantly asks the question, 'Why?'[27]

❏ *Responsibility for creation involves male-female co-partnership*

Filling the earth and subduing it can have another undesirable effect if done wrongly. The Bible asserts that the quality of our lives depends on our relationship to and knowledge of God the Father, Son and Holy Spirit. Those who choose, independently of God's power and wisdom in Christ (1 Corinthians 1, verse 24), to map their own path to the good life may fulfil some of their desires in this short life on earth; but in the life of the ages to come, such people face judgment because they failed to consult the right map.

They are like the Israelites in the time of the
judges, when 'all the people did what was right in
their own eyes' (Judges 21, verse 25); like Adam and
Eve who chose to set autonomous standards of wisdom and knowledge of good and evil, but who lost
so many privileges and blessings as a result — and
thus dealt a mortal blow to the human race. They
are like those who 'exchanged the truth about God
for a lie and worshipped and served the creature
rather than the creator' (Romans 1, verse 25). God
shows his people in the scriptures how to live within
his boundary lines, which gives purpose and fulfilment in the face of alluring but idolatrous forces
within a secular culture.

It is of fundamental importance to note the unity
of male and female in the task of replenishing and
controlling the resources of the universe. The idea
of sexuality in verses 26 to 28 is not associated with
either the idea of the 'image' or of 'dominion', but
with the 'larger theme of sustainability or fertility'.[28]
There is certainly a male-female distinction, but the
task of filling and subduing the earth is given to
both men and women. God did not command the
male to 'subdue' the earth and the female to 'be
fruitful and multiply'. There was a *twofold* task,
which both as equals had to perform.

The task would best be achieved when the
polarities and similarities of male and female com-
bined in harmony. The material resources necessary

for survival were given by God to the man and woman as food: seed-bearing plants and fruits (verse 29). Animals and birds would be generously provided for from the same source (see Psalm 104). This is in marked contrast to Mesopotamian religion, where humans supplied the gods with food.[29]

God contemplated his work (chapter 1, verse 31 to chapter 2, verse 4b)
❑ *God allocated space for reflection*
At the end of the sixth day, God contemplated his work with satisfaction: 'Indeed it was very good' (verse 31). Once the balance had been established, it was up to men and women to maintain it. So 'the heavens and the earth were finished, and all their multitude' (chapter 2, verse 1) and God ceased from all his work and 'rested on the seventh day'.

The sabbath is a central part of biblical religion, though not mentioned here by name. Lambert argues that the connotation of Hebrew and Babylonian terms for 'sabbath' is the completion of the moon's waxing.[30] The ten commandments justify the sabbath on the basis of God's completion of creation: 'That is why Yahweh has blessed the sabbath day and made it sacred' (Exodus 20, verses 8 to 11, NJB). The rest gave time to reflect on and enjoy the fruit of one's toil. It also fitted the pattern of opposites already noted — in this case the balance between productivity and re-creation.

The sabbath was from that moment onwards given special significance for the people of God. This was not in any dualistic sense of being holy while the other six days of work were somehow inferior in God's eyes. Rather, the sabbath was intended to provide peace for God's people to stand back from the burdensome toil and drudgery of their weekly labour in order to look ahead to a day when their work was done and they could enjoy its fruits in fellowship with God for all eternity. It is unusual for God to bless or hallow anything other than people, animals or plant life (always denoting fertility or prosperity). Wenham suggests that 'those who observe the sabbath will enjoy divine blessing in their lives'.[31]

❑ *God has an attitude of reflection*
This is indicated not only in his allocation of the seventh day, but also in the oft-repeated phrase in chapter 1, 'And God saw that it was good'. This clause, or its variant, occurs seven times in the chapter and is significant for a number of reasons.

First, it suggests that a fundamental part of the creative work of God involved some time out for critical reflection on his own activity in creation. It's almost as if, before going on to his next creative activity, he stops momentarily to assess or evaluate the effectiveness, appropriateness or orderliness of each phase of the process.

Second, if God the creator saw the importance of reflection on action and built it into his creative schedule, how much more might we his creatures benefit from such a discipline! It was only *after* six days of action followed by reflection on action that he took a whole day off from the active part of his work to reflect on its value in the wider creation program.

There needs to be a greater balance to our frenetic, driven, non-reflective lives in modern suburbia. I wonder how many of our schedules and priorities would change — and to what extent — if we took regular time out for evaluation and modification of our plans and programs as individuals, families, churches, governments, trade unions and businesses?

Third, if reflection is an important activity for God's human creation, that creation must have a reliable standard by which to measure the worth of things. *Humanism* and *rationalism* in their secular or atheistic forms, the forms which dominate Western civilisation and culture, place each individual in the position of judge of right and wrong, objecting strongly to any intrusion by external authority such as church tradition or revelation. Protagoras' statement 'Man is the measure of all things' epitomises this approach.

Pragmatism extends this approach by measuring all thought and behaviour in terms of consequences:

something is said to be true if it helps us in some way: you judge a belief by its effects.

The problem with such a philosophy of life is that it only leads to relativism and scepticism, because it implies the possibility of several different understandings of what is right or wrong, of what works or doesn't work on a variety of issues. If there is no source of wisdom outside the limits of our humanness and reason, there can be no certainty about anything. One rational person's view is as good as another's.

This logic takes you to the time of the Judges, where 'there was no king in Israel [and] all the people did what was right in their own eyes' (Judges 21, verse 25). God is the source and arbiter of truth; he alone knows what is right or wrong. When he judges something, like an act of creation, as 'good' or sets standards of conduct through the scriptures, by faith we must defer to his divine wisdom and adjust the pattern of our lives accordingly.

Fourth, the sabbath highlights a critical weakness in the church's life in the West today. To a large extent, the suburban church fails in both of the above-mentioned areas: on the one hand, it doesn't provide a forum for serious reflection on action for its worshippers; on the other, its educational strategy does not aim to train the faculties of Christians to 'distinguish good from evil' (Hebrews 5, verse 14) or to 'take every thought captive to obey Christ' (2

Corinthians 10, verse 5).

Instead of developing programs which allow for reflection on 'all the business of life' each week, most church programs measure loyalty to God in attendance at a smorgasbord of church activities. Operational effectiveness in most churches is measured quantitatively or organisationally, not qualitatively or organically. Getting people to attend meetings seems more important than helping to shape a Christian worldview, which can then act redemptively in such different spheres of life as law, politics, architecture, media, and the arts and sciences.

The character of God as creator
What does this material show us about God?
❏ *God is supreme and without competitors*
In ancient Near Eastern mythology, the sun, moon, sea and its monsters were all viewed as enemies of the gods. Here, they are part of his handiwork.

❏ *God's word is powerful and authoritative*
Only a divine word has the capacity always to bring into existence what it expresses. What God says 'is to be understood as a creative command, as a deed'.[33] Each creative command gives a purpose to each entity created, a goal to which God's word directs cosmic history. Nothing happens capriciously or by fate, but according to a coherent plan of God.[34]

❏ *God is a God of order*
He separates day from night, heaven from earth, work from rest, and delegates this ordering task to his representatives, whom he equips with his own image and with all the resources of creation.

❏ *God affirms creation as a source of blessing and*
  pleasure
'Fall/redemption' theology has diverted Christians from 'creation-blessing' theology. It is impossible to understand properly God's activity in the world of nature. But we do know that blessing was the purpose of creation and original blessing the basis of trust and faith.[35] Earthiness and sensuality are, contrary to Christian legalism and asceticism, the mechanism through which blessing and fertility can be celebrated.

Other biblical references to creation[36]

The Psalms give us the only response possible to such creativity: 'When I look at your heavens, the work of your fingers, the moon and the stars that you have established; what are human beings that you are mindful of them?' (Psalm 8, verses 3 and 4).

The sage testifies to God's wisdom: 'When [the Lord] established the heavens, I [wisdom] was there, when he drew a circle on the face of the deep, when he made firm the skies above, when he established

the fountains of the deep. . . when he marked out
the foundations of the earth, then I was beside him,
like a master worker; and I was daily his delight'
(Proverbs 8, verses 27 to 30).

Job repents 'in dust and ashes' before the overwhelming majesty of God's creation (Job 38, verse 1
to Job 42, verse 6).

Paul says God's 'eternal power and divine nature,
invisible though they are, have been. . . seen through
the things he has made' (Romans 1, verse 20).

The apostle John describes how the Word was
instrumental in the process of creation: 'In the beginning was the Word, and the Word was with God
and. . . was God. He was in the beginning with God.
All things came into being through him, and without
him not one thing came into being. . . In him was
life, and the life was the light of all people. The light
shines in the darkness, and the darkness did not overcome it' (John 1, verses 1 to 5).

Discussion questions

Talking it through

1 What do you imagine the world was like before God's creative command, 'Let there be light'? Try and describe it in concrete terms. Refer to chapter 1, verses 1 and 2.

2 Why do you think the words 'spirit', 'wind' and 'breath' are interchangeable in verse 2? Does it make any difference to the meaning of the passage?

3 What are some of the major differences between human and divine speech or words?

4 There is a clear, implied criticism of other (astral) deities in chapter 1, verses 14 to 18 and elsewhere in both Old and New Testaments. How should Christians respond to alternative religious ideas and, more specifically, to the resurgence of these old superstitions in the form of astrology, fertility cults and New Age religion?

5 The so-called 'prosperity doctrine' suggests that *material* blessings are a direct and normal outcome of obedient faith. What is a biblical view of blessing? See pages 24, 25 and 32.

6 Read through the list of other biblical references to creation (pages 36 and 37). What makes the doctrine of creation so impressive and relevant to our age?

Widening our horizons

1 What light, if any, do the various branches of modern science throw on the idea of creation in Genesis 1? Why has the whole creation/evolution debate been something of a red herring?

2 What impact might belief in the doctrine of creation have on:
  * personal existence and well-being?
  * an understanding of primeval history?
  * sexual practices in society today?
  * contemporary scientific enterprise?
  * current ecological concerns?
  * religious experience?
    Does it matter if a personal God was not involved in creation?

3 'An arrogant and triumphalist view of the place of humans in the order of creation. Small wonder the world is in the mess it's in!' How might Christians respond to such a criticism of Genesis 1, verses 26 to 28?

4 Why has the biblical tradition of the 'sabbath'

lost some of its force or relevance among
Christians in our secular society? How
might its meaning be restored within the:
* local church?
* Christian home?
* secular world?
* office or manufacturing plant?

5 If God created all humans (male and female,
rich and poor, black and white) in his own
image, how is it that so much sexism, racism
and classism have flourished within the Christian church over the centuries — not just in
the wider community? (Don't just describe
this as 'sin'. Think deeper. *Why* can't we
tolerate human difference?)

   Why does the whole notion of diversity
rub against the grain of our human nature?

2
Forging and breaking bonds

What was God's purpose for his creation?
GENESIS CHAPTER 2, VERSE 4B TO
CHAPTER 3, VERSE 24

THIS PASSAGE APPEARS TO BE separate from the earlier creation narrative. It is a story that was originally passed down orally, like similar stories about creation, evil, suffering and death. There is a deliberate sequence that begins, Claus Westermann says, with 'the command that God gives to his human creatures, and ascends to a climax with the transgression of the command. It then descends. . . to the consequences of the transgression — the discovery, the trial and the punishment. The conclusion. . . expulsion from the garden. . . calls to mind the beginning.'[1]

Genesis 2 and 3 differ from Genesis 1 in three ways. First, whereas the later chapters are a prelude to God's activity among Israel — his people — Genesis 1 is more concerned with God's *cosmic* activity. Second, the later chapters are more concerned with 'the forging of bonds: between man and soil, man and the animals, man and woman, man and God',[2] whereas Genesis 1 is more concerned with distinction and separation.

Third, the name *Yahweh Elohim*, 'the Lord God', occurs twenty times in these later chapters, but once only elsewhere (in Exodus 9, verse 30, where the text is unclear), whereas *Elohim*, 'God', is used in chapter 1. The two names — *Yahweh Elohim* — are probably linked to draw together the two names, *Elohim* in chapter 1 and *Yahweh* in much of the rest of the Pentateuch. It is likely, Gordon Wenham thinks, that the author of chapter 2 (probably different from that of chapter 1) 'deliberately used [*Yahweh Elohim*] to express his conviction that *Yahweh* is both Israel's covenant partner and the God, *Elohim*, of all creation'.[3]

The context: a desert
(chapter 2, verses 4b to 7)

As with the first 3 verses of Genesis 1, the action is set against a context of 'not-yet-ness' (verses 4b to 6).

Gerhard von Rad suggests that, whereas in

Genesis 1 the context was chaos-cosmos, in chapter 2 the context was desert-earth.[4] Wenham states that instead of a watery chaos before God's word-action of creation in chapter 1, chapter 2 sees the whole earth as a desert.[5]

The apparent contradiction between verse 5 (no rain or vegetation) and verse 6 (a great spring from the underground ocean that watered the earth) can be resolved if the absence of human activity ('no one to till the soil') is seen as the reason for withholding water before God's creative work in verse 7. This is the main clause, a climax to verse 4b onwards, which is meant to be seen as necessitating the coming of water.

Verse 7 refers to our 'dustness', a characteristic of humankind taken up in Job 10, verse 9; Isaiah 29, verse 16; and Psalm 104, verse 29. Of the forty-six references to *adam* in Genesis 1 to 11, all refer to the 'creation of humanity and the limitations of the human state',[6] our 'dustness'. The book of Ecclesiastes focuses on the fragility and mortality of humanity as such — 'all is nothingness'. Genesis 2, verse 7, while stressing the distinctiveness of humanity, also provides a balance to the royal dignity and godlike qualities of chapter 1 by underlining our 'dustness'. Here humans are dependent creatures, made out of perishable material.

In contrast to the more lofty and idealistic view of chapter 1, the emphasis here seems to be on the limitation, creatureliness and dependence of humans. The apparent word-play — *adam* means 'man' and *adamah* means 'ground' — suggests that 'human beings and earth belong together, that the earth is there for humanity and human beings are there to populate it.'[7] As Gunkel says, 'Man is created from the ground and he is called to till the ground; his dwelling is on the ground and he returns to the ground when he dies.'[8]

The 'breath of life' (verse 7) refers to the fact that God made the man come alive: until that point, his was an inanimate body. Von Rad reminds us that 'the undertone of melancholy is unmistakeable: a faint anticipation of the state of post-Adamic man! When God withdraws his breath (Psalm 104, verse 29f; Job 34, verse 14f), man reverts to dead corporeity.'[9] And so the full status and dignity of humans is reached: 'So man became a living person.'

The word *nephesh* can mean 'appetite, throat, person, soul, self, corpse'. Even if 'soul' is used (as in the AV and the RV), one cannot argue that the soul is put into the body, or that a person is made up of a body and a soul — the word *nephesh* cannot be defined tightly enough for that.

In the desert, a garden
(chapter 2, verses 8 and 9)
Having formed and fashioned the man, God now provides for his sustenance. The garden — a

parkland or fertile orchard surrounded by a hedge — seems to be mysteriously located somewhere 'in the east', in Mesopotamia or Arabia. The mystical word *paradise* comes from a Greek translation of the Hebrew word 'garden'. The word *Eden* means 'pleasure, delight, bliss'.[10] Wherever it is mentioned, it is a fertile, well-watered oasis with large trees.

But God sets limits for his creation; man is placed in the garden to await instructions (verse 15). The resources for his nourishment were provided in the garden. The sight, taste, touch and smell of the orchard affirm things of beauty, rich to the senses. There is an innocence here but, with the tree of knowledge of good and evil, also the possibility of loss of innocence.

The 'tree of life' (verse 9) was well-known in Ancient Israel and belongs to the mythology of the ancient Near East — the *Gilgamesh Epic* has a reference to a plant conferring eternal youth — and stems from the universal fear of death and the belief that eternal life was unattainable.[11]

The 'tree of the knowledge of good and evil' (verse 9) has been interpreted in various ways: the mysterious secrets of life, scientific understanding of skills and the uses of nature, sexual awareness, moral discernment or autonomy, independent discrimination, omniscience, wisdom.[12] Some calculate the age of knowledge of good and evil as the time of weaning (about three years old in the Semitic world); the

Qumran community set it at the 'age of sufficient maturity to make communal decisions'. In the tree of the knowledge of good and evil, we have at core the idea of moral autonomy where humans — independent of God — seek to determine whether a thing is good or not.[13]

The tree of life offered immortality, whereas the tree of the knowledge of good and evil offered experiences and knowledge 'appropriate only to the divine'.[14] It would seem that the 'test' of faith lay in the choice to let God's wisdom, and the boundaries of reality which he defines, govern human conduct and thought. Life could only be enjoyed by humans if they accepted reality as given. The tragedy was that the delights of Eden and the enjoyment of God and his creation could have been experienced if such boundaries had been honoured.

The garden is the centre of the world and may be symbolic of the king in his sanctuary.[15] The biblical notion of *knowledge*, contrary to Graeco-Roman concepts, involved experience; it was never simply an intellectual processing of facts. True Christian maturity involves having one's 'faculties trained by practice to distinguish good from evil' (Hebrews 5, verse 14).

And in the garden, a river
(chapter 2, verses 10 to 14)

We are suddenly moved out of the human story into

a historical and geographical world. In a sort of echo of the city with its river 'whose streams make glad the city of God' (Psalm 46, verse 4), this river that waters the parkland orchard is described as the source of the rivers that water the world. Westermann says that the intention of the author was not to determine where paradise lay, but to point out that the 'life arteries' of all lands of the earth have their source in the river that watered paradise.[16]

After leaving the garden, the river divided into four 'branches', a puzzling description of the four largest river systems in the ancient world. There is certainly no agreement as to the identity of the first two branches, Pishon and Gihon. Havilah, the 'land of sand', may have been in Arabia which was known for its gold.

Bdellium (verse 12) is a sort of resin or transparent gum-like wax. Onyx stone is a type of gem used for decorating the tabernacle and temple and in the high-priestly vestments.[17]

Cush (verse 13) usually refers to Ethiopia, though in Genesis 10, verse 8, it means the Cassites — successors of the Old Babylonian empire in Western Iran. As far as the location of Eden is concerned, no conclusion has been drawn to the debate: some suggest a Mesopotamian site; others, somewhere in Armenia near the sources of the Tigris and Euphrates; others, near the head of the Persian Gulf, where three of the rivers converge.

Walter Brueggemann designates the relationship between humans in the garden and God as 'vocation, permission and prohibition':[18]

❑ *Vocation*

The purpose of existence in the garden was not self-indulgent pleasure, but work defined as caring for and guarding the parkland orchard. Here is no undervaluing of manual work as against intellectual or aesthetic activity. Work is an essential ingredient for all meaningful human activity. The word for 'to till' (literally 'to serve') refers to manual work and religious worship; the word 'to keep' or 'guard' concerns both 'sacred' and 'secular' activity.[19]

The notion of the king as gardener occurs in Mesopotamian royal ideology; Nicholas Wyatt points out that Adam in this sense represents a king. Care for the environment has a dignity and is linked to the reference to the 'dominion' and 'subjection' of the earth. John Macquarrie makes a distinction between 'monarchical' and 'organic' humanism, the former 'makes man the measure of all things and sets the world over against him'; the latter is more aware of 'man's affinity with the world. . . to which he owes a responsibility as yet undefined'.[20]

In Sumerian and Babylonian creation myths, humans were created to relieve the gods of their burdens. Work is part of being human. It is tragic when the opportunity to explore and manage the earth's resources is either denied — as in unemployment, corruption or imprisonment — or abused through exploitation, workaholism or mismanagement.

❏ Permission

The right to eat freely from the garden was a blessing from God, involving fruitfulness and freedom. There was to be no lack of food or resources, for all people equally could enjoy life in communion with God and each other. Of concern, therefore, is the unequal access to and distribution of material resources at a global level.

To use the images of balance and order from Genesis 1, we could argue that to cultivate and guard the earth means to work and rest it so that all, not just the privileged, benefit. A 'liberationist' reading of this text offers a corrective to the traditional interpretation, which looks at reality from the perspective of power, wealth and status. Here lies the prophetic challenge to all structures — local, national and global — that cream off material wealth at the expense of the majority of humanity.

❏ Prohibition

This needs to be set against the background of the two prior blessings: the divine call to work in the parkland and the provision of resources to fulfil such a task. The threat of death, if taken literally, did not come to fruition for over 900 years for Adam, according to chapter 5, verse 5.

The reason for the command is not given; it simply defines the boundaries within which humans can enjoy the blessedness of life. The idea behind the 'tree of the knowledge of good and evil' is probably that of choice or the 'knowledge of possibilities'.[21] Westermann says, 'to say no to God — and this is what freedom allows — is ultimately to say no to life; for life comes from God'.[22] True freedom only exists where clear limits are established. Any society which rejects the constraints of traditional morality or social limits on individual freedom, can no longer be a true community or have a relationship with God.

The rejection of God's authority and wisdom, which lies at the heart of the temptation in chapter 3, leads to a return to primeval chaos for human civilisation — the disintegration of all living relationships. When a human being or nation venerates its own wisdom and rejects God's, then personal alienation, social *anomie* and cosmic destruction are the inevitable consequences: death on a macro scale!

The formation of the woman (chapter 2 verses 18 to 25)

We come now to an apparent contradiction of chapter 1, verse 31 — that everything God made, male and female included, was 'very good'. There is still an incompleteness requiring a new creative decision by God — 'I will make him a helper as his partner.' The recognition of the initial inadequacy of the creation of human beings serves to highlight the fact that there is something special about humans.

To realise one's potential, one must be part of a community. Having noted the inadequacy in creation, God intervenes by making a 'helper complementary to him' or, as Walsh says, a matching helper.[23] The meaning of 'help' goes beyond the idea of help in work or in procreation to the notion of mutual assistance in the broadest sense. Irenaeus understood 'helper' to mean one of superior strength. Most occurrences of the word refer to help from a stronger, not weaker person.[24]

As 'dustness' conveys the sense of fragility, 'dependence' becomes part of human existence. The woman corresponds to man as his counterpart. There is a suspenseful pause between the decision to provide a helper and the fulfilment of the promise, which highlights loneliness as a human problem.

No mention has been made of animal and bird life: can they serve as man's helpers or companions? After all, according to verse 7, they are formed from the ground as humans were. By bringing them to the man for naming, God was allowing him to discover what sort of companion suited him best.

The act of naming amounts to the discovery and ordering of reality — not that man created it. The curiosity and analysis involved in the process lie at the heart of learning and scientific enterprise. By exploring creation in this way, and unlocking its secrets, humans are fulfilling the cultural mandate undergirding all intellectual and social activity throughout history. Here we have an indirect affirmation of science, technology, the arts, the social sciences, business management — of all quests for meaning and order.

The phrase 'one flesh' (verse 24) is a formula of relationship used to denote a permanent tie of kinship.[25] Humanity reaches its goal in the complementary relationship and mutuality between man and woman. Naming needn't denote power over the thing named, as some commentators suggest, simply the interpreting and discerning of reality — giving those named a meaning.

The reference to leaving (verse 24) highlights the new relationship between a man and his wife: such is the force of his love that it draws him away from the only ties he has known, with parents. In the Semitic culture, a man didn't leave his parents' household, but continued to live in or near it. A better translation is 'forsake', which highlights the shift of loyalties in setting up a new household. Many marriages run into difficulties because ties with parents have not been adjusted by the newlywed(s).

The idea of cleaving to one's spouse has the sense

of a covenant bond for life. Shechem's soul (Genesis 34, verse 3) is said to have 'stuck' to Dinah; Israel was urged to 'stick by' Yahweh (Deuteronomy 10, verse 20). The comparison is made by the prophet in Jeremiah 3, verses 1 onwards, between Israel's 'whoring' after other gods and the 'marriage' to Yahweh, where righteousness is measured in terms of loyalty to given relationships — God, spouse, children, master, neighbour.

Becoming 'one flesh' (verse 24) is a consequence of the two prior relational commitments — leaving and cleaving. The context for a fulfilling sexual relationship is marriage, where two people make a clear break — emotionally, socially, economically — from primary parental bonds, and covenant together to be loyal to each other and to their Lord for the rest of their lives. Such an understanding needs to be underlined in marriage preparation classes and Christian Education programs. The deception today is that immediate sexual gratification leads to happiness and that sex is a mere biological function, similar to hunger and thirst.

Nakedness (verse 25) is set in the context of the marriage relationship and is not generalised here or elsewhere in the Bible to imply acceptance of communal practices such as nude bathing or going without clothes. The privacy of marriage is a proper backdrop for such intimate self-disclosure. It can be inferred that other occasions for 'nudity', apart from particular tribal customs, or in childhood or for medical examinations, is a thing of 'shame'. To be without shame is to be less than human — especially where a wrong has been committed — for such shame can result in a turning away from sin. This has implications for the portrayal of the naked human body in film, photography, theatre, advertising, painting and the arts.

The man-woman community relationship that is exemplified in these verses provides a model in some ways for community relationships in general. Yet many of our relationships today work in a way quite different from that envisaged in these verses. Competitiveness and individualism seem to go hand in hand in modern urban societies. Because of alienation from our Maker, we seek fulfilment in relationships of *domination* — over the material and social world — rather than through cooperation.

Winning is seen as the mark of success in politics, business and sport. The message of the daily media — news stories, film, pop music, radio and especially advertising — is that the 'most important person in the world is *you*'. The only absolute law left, if 'God is dead', is the law of enlightened individualism: 'Providing my behaviour doesn't interfere with anyone else's freedom or well-being, I can do what I like.'

The bottom line is simply *worship of the self* which permeates the thinking of many, even in the so-called 'helping' professions; it is the credo of many marketing and advertising strategies; and it underlies assumptions about our incontestable right to such privileges as owning a gun, house or car.

A biblical perspective, however, puts the emphasis on *interdependence* and community. Genesis 2 makes it clear that 'going it alone' is contrary to God's will for the human race. We were meant, from creation onwards, to work together as equal partners and share the fruits of our toil across all boundaries of age, sex, class, ethnicity and culture. In Jesus Christ such barriers have been broken once and for all, as Galatians 3, verse 28 indicates very clearly.

The Christian church ought to be part of the solution to the alienation and loneliness of our technological society. Unfortunately, it often — at least in the West — is part of the problem. Once the organic self-understanding of the New Testament church was displaced by institutional and hierarchical models (in the third and fourth centuries), the individual member tended to get swept aside by the demands of a clerical style of leadership, with decision-making, liturgy, instruction and ministry all in the hands of a few 'professionals'.

It is common for gifted, loyal and intelligent lay people in today's church to feel alienated by the structures, decision-making systems, even the worship and educational processes. Power has been concentrated for so long in the hands of clergy plus a privileged lay oligarchy that little changes in the way God's work is done.

The main tasks for local church members continue to be, as they always have been, to attend weekly services and support the church financially — to pay, pray and obey. The church offering enables the paid leadership to live independent lives like the laity, but such financial security paradoxically disempowers most clergy from engaging in a truly biblical and prophetic ministry. The relationship between priest and parishioner should be one of economic inter-dependence.

Rather than the golden calf of financial inde-pendence, we should be encouraging the pooling of material and human resources — wages, property, skills, time — for the benefit of the community and the kingdom of God: locally, nationally and globally. But the problem of *competitive individualism* — rein-forced through TV, radio, magazines — instead reigns supreme in most suburban churches, where lonely people look in vain for companionship, or the disempowered for justice.

God's twofold mandate: community and order in creation

We now pull together the threads from chapters 1 and 2 and look at the twofold mandate God has given humankind.

❏ *Community*

The first mandate is that we are made to create community. Because it was 'not good that the man should be alone', God's original mandate for Adam and Eve was to 'fill' the earth, 'be fruitful and multiply'; and for the institution of marriage to provide the social structure for such relationships — a point made in chapter 2, verse 24.

The characteristics of this redemptive community are numerous and include righteousness, justice, truth, peace and mercy.

(a) Love for God

People remain faithful to the many and varied sets of relationships in which God places them. Loyalty to God governs everything: obligations to state, spouse and family, employer, or friend.

(b) Love of neighbour

God made all persons — male and female, Jew and Greek, peasant and aristocrat — in his image and likeness, to serve and honour him through the gifts each has. The kind of relationships which preserve social order and harmony are those which honour each individual as bearer of that divine likeness and character, but which also recognise the destructive force of human sinfulness.

Making this community redemptive in today's pluralistic world will involve us in two courses of action, one negative, one positive. First, we need to take a prophetic and critical stance against life-denying models of human relationships — at home, in the media, at work, and through unjust social policies or global inequalities. Christians should be advocates for social justice at all levels, simply because God hates all dehumanising relationships. See Deuteronomy 10, verses 12 to 22; Isaiah 58; Matthew 25, verses 31 to 46; James 1, verse 27 to chapter 2, verse 17.

Second, there is a need for Christians to develop new ways of modelling kingdom values within local communities. Unfortunately, contemporary social research shows very little difference between the life values of church- and non-churchgoers.[26] If the latter see Christians pursuing material aggrandisement and social status or getting involved in immorality and corruption, then it is small wonder they can't see how Christianity makes for a better society.

❑ *Order in creation*
The second mandate is that we are made to maintain his world of order.

God's work of creation involved shaping the pre-existent, chaotic watery mass through his creative word (Genesis 1, verses 1 to 3). He separated light from darkness, the waters above from those below the heavens, day from night, earth from ocean, humans from animals, birds and fish. By making mortals in his image and likeness, he equipped them for a kind of enterprise with him as 'senior partner', which carried on where his original creative work left off. As male and female, they had different primary gifts and motivations; but both joined together with God as equal partners in the following activities:

(a) Naming the animals

This involved all the processes we now regard as part of the modern scientific enterprise — observation, analysis, replication, description, hypothesis- and theory-building. The picture is a clear affirmation of all scientific activity. The huge difference between this and modern science is that here in Genesis, science is a response to the divine call to order and manage the creation, never an end in itself or even a means to an end — such as the glorification of autonomous human reason.

The biblical model suggests that humans are called by God to the scientific task so that, with him, they might enjoy the blessings within creation more fully and thus bring glory to his name.

(b) Cultivating the garden

Humans are made from and for the earth. Their fragility as dust and their calling as caretakers of Eden serve as a salutary reminder that, compared with God the creator who is Lord of culture and of history, mere mortals owe their very breath to God.

The notion of 'guarding' and 'cultivating' the garden suggests that, because we depend for our livelihood on the earth's productivity, we ought to look after it properly and not abuse it or pollute it in any way. It is God's gracious gift to us to enjoy. Our toil and sweat in keeping out the weeds ought to remind us that this activity is never an end in itself, but a means to the wider purpose of enjoying God — by productively managing his creation and providing for our daily bread.

(c) *Subduing the earth, having dominion over the fish, the birds and all living things*
While mortals have in one sense a lowly part to play in the work of God's kingdom, they also have a majestic or kingly role. The amazing aspect of this truth is in contrast to other creation stories in Mesopotamia, where humans are created merely to feed or entertain the gods.

On the one hand, humans must give due acknowledgment to God's majesty, power and glory, by admitting their dependence on him for life, fruitfulness and wisdom — the point of the tree of knowledge of good and evil. But, on the other, they have a magnificent status of 'priestly royalty' (Exodus 19, verse 6) whose task is to reconcile all things in creation to God.

*   *   *

No-one likes to be told what to do or how to do it. Genesis 3 provides theological insights into what happens when humans refuse to live within the boundaries designated by God. It highlights the subtle stages by which we rationalise our own self-willed behaviour and refuse to take responsibility for it. It shows how one act of self-will makes the next one easier but also more necessary if we need to cover our tracks.

The remainder of the Bible is a response to what happens in this brief but devastating encounter between responsible humans and a God who, by very nature, retains the right to set boundaries within which humans must operate if their enterprises are to prosper. To reflect on this story is to reflect on one's own struggle to operate successfully in life.

The crime that broke the bond
(chapter 3, verses 1 to 7)

Dietrich Bonhoeffer describes the encounter between snake and woman as the 'first conversation *about* God'.[27]

We are told that the snake was 'more crafty than any other wild animal God had made' (verse 1). Several suggestions about the identity of the snake have been offered over the centuries. People have thought it represents:

* *Satan in disguise.* This needs to be balanced against the more positive understanding of the saving power of the serpent in the wilderness and its direct comparison, in John 3, with the lifting up of the Son of Man.

* *Human or intellectual curiosity.* Under this interpretation, the snake is a projection of Eve's thought processes, an externalisation of her quest for knowledge.

* *A mythical being.* Here, the Israelite tradition is reduced to a magical creature — the occult source of hidden wisdom or vitality that brought prosperity. In Canaanite cultic tradition, the serpent helps the goddess as 'fertiliser, life-giver, life-renewer, restorer'.[28] Those that believe this to be the correct interpretation say that in this passage there is a condemnation of all forms of magical knowledge or encounters.

* *An evil demon.* Another view is that the snake was an evil demon, hostile to God and humanity, that brought life and death, belonged to chaos, was a god of the underworld, but which was reduced in Israelite traditions to an animal.[29]

* *A clever animal that could speak.* This interpretation is difficult if the serpent is one of God's 'good' creatures.

There seems to be more at work in the story than

merely what is suggested by the second or fifth explanations. I prefer the earlier form of the third interpretation.

There are three stages in the temptation narrative:

❑ *Reduction of the divine name*
The name *Yahweh* was changed by the serpent and then by Eve (verse 3) to the more remote and less personal form *Elohim*. Theologically, *Elohim* denotes God as creator, while *Yahweh* was the term for a personal, covenant-making deity.

Sin is viewed by the author of Genesis as a demonic force arising out of, as Childs writes, 'an incomprehensible hatred toward God which revolts against his authority'.[29] Our view of God is critical in our determining how we should live; once that view is reduced or altered, one becomes vulnerable to the subtle allurements of other claims on one's loyalty.

This process is not confined to a God-denying, agnostic, secular culture! It is disturbing to see how many churches portray a deity that fulfils people's private needs and makes them feel happy at the expense of other less 'comforting' attributes, such as holiness, justice, mystery and hiddenness.

❑ *Playing down or ignoring of God's generosity*
Here, God is portrayed as a kind of 'party pooper' who is out to trip us up. His intentions are ques-

tioned — in effect, 'Maybe he's frightened you'll challenge his power and status' — and the attractiveness of autonomy, divinity and wisdom is asserted in verse 5.

The appeal of the senses is noted in verse 6: food, there to be eaten, looked so attractive and could unlock the mysteries of the world!

❏ *Inclusion of her mate in the process*
Possibly to cover herself in case of discovery, Eve implicates Adam as a partner in crime (verse 6)! There is no suggestion of seduction by the wife. As Westermann wryly comments: 'No temptation was needed in the case of the man; he simply fell into line.'[30]

The couple got more than they bargained for. Their eyes certainly were opened: they discovered new things about themselves which they didn't enjoy and tried to deal with them somewhat ineptly (verse 7). The reason for overstepping the boundaries was a basic human urge, Westermann says, to explore the 'new possibilities of life that are apparently opened by the transgression'.[31]

The consequences of breaking the bond (chapter 3, verses 8 to 24)

These fall into four groups: fear and guilt, accusation and suspicion, curses and finally exile:

❑ *Fear and guilt (verses 8 to 11)*
Human disobedience, ingratitude and pride created
a rift in the relationship between the primal couple
and God.

The picture of fellowship as a walk with God —
in this case through a garden — is one that recurs
throughout the scriptures. The tragedy of Adam
and Eve was that their guilt profoundly distorted
that fellowship, causing them to withdraw from
God's presence. The absurdity was that they
thought they could hide from the creator behind the
things he'd created! Guilt led to a distortion of
reality.

One interpretation that has been given of the
question, 'Where are you?' (verse 9) is that God had
limited himself to the cognitive boundaries of mere
human existence and didn't know where the man
and his wife were or that they were actually hiding
from him. But this defies reason: God must have
known exactly where the pair was — physically and
spiritually. He wanted them to identify where they
were in relation to him.

A grasp of reality can only occur when a proper
answer to this question is given by all human beings
— first, in regard to our primary relationship with
God; then, in regard to one's personal and social
identity. True humanness can only occur when
relationships flow out of a union with the One who
formed us in his own image. God was aware of

the rift in the relationship and the consequent guilt and fear; it was part of his nature to pursue the relationship and to give them a chance to declare themselves in their alienation and brokenness — to invite mercy and reconciliation at their point of vulnerability and need.

The man had no prior knowledge of how God would react to his disobedience, only the fear of death itself: 'On the day you eat. . . you will surely die.' The earliest human emotion recorded in the narrative (sadly) is that of fear, linked to the realisation of nakedness — once symbolic of openness and innocence, but now of vulnerability. The body was originally a measure of intimacy and sexual fulfilment within the marriage relationship. Because of alienation from God, however, we have found ways of using it to advance our own pleasures, generally at the expense of women, but more recently, with devastating impact, in the global spread of AIDS.

From the transgressor's viewpoint here, God is to be feared as adversary or judge. The terror of judgment by a holy God is symbolised in the feeble attempt to hide from his presence behind fig leaves.

❏ *Accusation and suspicion (verses 12 and 13)*
The man refused to take responsibility for his action, shifting the blame first to God — 'the woman *you* gave me' — then to the one previously acknowledged as an appropriate partner. We see the moral

immaturity which is characteristic of sin: the natural tendency to justify or exonerate ourselves by making others look worse than we are. Comparisons with others may appear to let us off the hook, but not in front of a holy God.

Implicit here is a deep, possibly universal male suspicion and fear of woman as seducer. In Israel and ancient Near Eastern societies, men had the responsible decision-making roles politically as elders, judges and monarchs and then ecclesiastically throughout Christendom. It explains some of the sexual inequality in ancient and modern societies. Even the apostle Paul (in 1 Timothy 2, verses 9 to 15, compare Ecclesiasticus 25, verse 24) based his argument for male authority structures in the church on the myth of the fickleness and gullibility of women.

Our interpretation of Genesis 1 to 11 has focussed on the notion of creation as the ordering of the chaotic and of harmonising such opposites as light-darkness, male-female, work-rest, earth-heavens and land-sea. By polarising opposites (male *versus*female), and denying the value of one over against the other — rather than drawing on the strengths of both to create harmony — we miss out on the wholeness and creativity that God originally intended.

❑ *Curses (verses 14 to 19)*
The first curse, the punishment on the serpent, is

described in terms of its position of vulnerability to attack — though this hardly seems to single the serpent out as more accursed than any other animals. The snake, apart from its physical lowness and inferiority, is humiliated further by having to eat dust and crawl at the feet of humans (verse 14).

More allegorical or Christological interpretations have been read into this passage: Christ is the woman's offspring, Satan is the serpent's brood, with ultimate victory belonging to Christ who receives temporary or minor wounds only.

However, we should look for the author's intention instead of reading modern agendas back into the material. The woman's offspring (verse 15) is literally the rest of human civilisation. There may be a hint of sinister forces in the snake, in the light of snake mythology: hence the perennial and damaging struggle between humans and the demonic or life-denying forces in the world.

The period curse and pain in childbirth already existed for the woman; the consequence of disobedience was the *increase* of her pain and lack of fulfilment within marriage (verse 16). The fact that the core of her being as mother and wife was affected, was central to the curse.

Eve's relationship with her husband (verse 17) will now be more vulnerable to abuse and domination as a result of alienation from God and her relative physical inferiority. Note that God is not *prescribing* domination; it is a simple statement of fact — the consequence of sin.

There will be agony and ecstasy within the marital bond — a yearning for a deeply satisfying communion of equals that will only partially or fleetingly be fulfilled. On the other hand, domination and oppression will be more characteristic of the relationship. The companion of chapter 2 has become a master.[33] It will be only through Jesus, the second Adam, that this inequality and oppression will be overturned.

The mistake the man makes is to accept his wife's offer of the forbidden fruit; he took heed of the wrong word. The second Adam resisted a similar temptation with the right word: 'One does not live by bread alone, but by every word that comes from the mouth of God,' said Jesus. Idolatry always involves this rejection of God's wisdom — in creation, in revelation and in Christ.

We all want to do what is right in our own eyes, according to our own autonomous human reason. Faith should have dismissed immediately the doubt in Adam and Eve's minds about God's wisdom and generosity, provoked by the serpent's taunts. Instead, 'unbelief' nurtured the possibility.

The curse against the man is indirect: what should have been a pleasure-giving activity — cultivating the ground for its food, energy and life — now takes on the form of a life-and-death struggle for survival, to which all humans will succumb (verses 17 and 18). The earth will now yield its fruit reluctantly and only after endless toil.

The whole of life will be given over to fatigue-ridden, futile or frustrating labour, merely for the human race to survive. Work will carry within it an alienating function; the earth over which God gave humans authority and dominion is now the conqueror (verse 19). A sobering reality emerges for post-Eden civilisation: work for mere survival's sake becomes part-and-parcel of the human struggle. Weeds in the garden speak of our vulnerability as well as the need for constant effort!

'Dust you are' (verse 19) seems to contradict the loftier view of human life expressed in chapter 1, verse 26 onwards. *Both* perspectives are true and should be held in tension: we are made in the image and likeness of God, but are also creatures of dust. This corrects any illusion about our origins and purpose on this earth and is one of the strongest reminders of human fragility, dependence and mortality.

❏ *Exile (verses 20 to 24)*
The husband recognises that his wife is bearer and nurturer of life. The distinctive gift God has given her — and all women — is to establish and sustain community. When all hope in the human enterprise disappeared, a woman is singled out as the means

by which life and not death would triumph (verse 20).

This pivotal role in community-creating is assigned to one woman — and to all women through her — in God's plan for the restoration of life in a world that is destructive of life. Note the roles of Sarah (Genesis 21, verses 1 and 2), Hannah (1 Samuel 1, verse 20), Elizabeth (Luke 1, verse 13) and Mary (Matthew 1, verse 18) later in the Bible. The affirmation and nourishment of life and peace through these women must never be underestimated as a force for social harmony.

The picture in verse 21 is a dramatic demonstration of a gracious and accommodating God. The man and his partner have failed to cover their guilt and shame through their nakedness. God accepts them in their vulnerability when he might well have left them exposed, but at a substantial cost to his creation. Human guilt or sin is 'covered over' with the skins of innocent animals that pay the ultimate sacrifice for someone else's disobedience.

Here is a foreshadowing of the later theology of atonement — more focussed under Moses, but only fulfilled in Christ's atoning sacrifice. The point of this story is that it is God's nature to overlook our sinfulness, but at a price — the death of an innocent victim. But God still invites us in all our flawedness to join forces in fellowship and service with him.

For any who 'dethrone' God, their privileges will

be curtailed. They will lose access to and partnership with God and enjoyment of the life-giving resources of his domain — Eden. The man and woman are banished from the garden to prevent them from tasting of the tree of life and living forever. By eating from the forbidden tree, they entered into the realm of good and evil. Once the possibility opened up for humans to decide for themselves what was good or bad and to pursue evil freely, to live forever would multiply the force of evil infinitely. Never to be able to escape from such bondage would be a curse.

The scripture documents the way God provides a path back into Eden and a life of fellowship with and service to the creator. The potential for self-destruction lies in the knowledge of good and evil as well as the possibility of eternal life. There can only be one source of wisdom and life; this story asserts where that source lies.

We need fear no evil, because God relinquishes his sovereignty to no-one. He is the author and judge of life. The mystery of faith lies in the gospel call here to all humans to let God take his rightful place. There is no other way of access to the tree of life.

Discussion questions

Talking it through

1 In what important ways does the story of creation in Genesis 2 and 3 differ from that of Genesis 1?

2 God must have known his prohibition in chapter 2, verse 16 would provoke a sinful reaction by the two humans. To what extent should God be held responsible for the consequences?

3 What model of marriage is given in chapter 2, verse 24 (compare this with chapter 10, verses 6 to 9)? Why do so many Christian marriages fail? See especially pages 53 and 54 (section on 'leaving').

4 How have Christians tended to react to nudity and semi-nakedness? What do you think is a Christian approach to nudity:
(a) in film, theatre or dance?
(b) in advertising?

(c) in public places?
(d) in the family home?

5 What do you think about the author's
criticism of the contemporary church (pages
56 to 57)? Do you agree/disagree? Is the
ideal of economic interdependence (page 57)
a practicable one?

6 'He will be your master' (chapter 3, verse 6).
Does this view support male headship within
both the home and the church? Does the
fact that the verse is a curse affect how we
use it?

Widening our horizons

1 'Dust you are, to dust you will return' (Genesis 3, verse 19): the biblical idea has as an important element the dependence, fragility and mortality of human nature. What aspects of modern society deny this fragility or anaesthetise our consciousness from its pain?

2 Chapter 2, verse 9 mentions the garden as 'pleasing to the eye'. Yet Jesus said if our eyes cause us to sin, we should pluck them out (Matthew 5, verse 29); John talked about the 'lust of the eyes' (1 John 2, verse 16). How is it possible to enjoy the beauty of creation without being lured into sin by its various images (on screen, in print or in the flesh)?

3 Today, many newly marrieds have to live in the home of one of their parents — normally the bride's — whilst they become financially independent. How can issues like emotional independence, privacy and the integrity of the individual marriage relationship be resolved?

4 Modern Western societies are saturated with explicit sexual images — an affront to people from more modest, sexually-reticent cultures and offensive to older, more conservative citizens. Artists and photographers often focus on the human body in terms of its aesthetic beauty.

How can we approve what is good without reverting to prudery on the one hand or titillation on the other? At what point does freedom of expression become a form of sexual exploitation?

5 Paul argues that because the woman was deceived (not the man), women mustn't teach or have leadership over men in the church (1 Timothy 2, verse 11 to 15). Is it possible to place a high value on the Bible, but disagree with Paul on the role of women in the church? If so, how? If not, why not?

6 How accurate is Genesis 3's diagnosis of the human condition? Where does it offer hope? What does it suggest are central problem areas? What are the human roots of conflict, oppression, alienation and dehumanisation?

3
Social order and disorder

*How did God's original plan
come unstuck?*
GENESIS CHAPTER 4, VERSE 1 TO
CHAPTER 5, VERSE 32

GENESIS 1 TO 3 PORTRAYS THE EVENTS of creation
and fall with a focus on two individuals who had
the potential for either fellowship with or inde-
pendence from God. Choosing independence
brought for them several unexpected consequences:
alienation from God and a deep sense of shame and
guilt in his presence; division and mistrust between
the primal couple, with the likelihood of male
dominance; toil and frustration in work; a hostile
environment; and, for the woman, a sharp increase

in the pain of childbirth.

The message of the writer so far is that God is good and that his creation, symbolised by Eden, has within it resources for an effective life, for developing community and for managing God's world.

The only way true life and blessedness can be enjoyed is if humans keep within God's boundaries. The potential for a return to primeval chaos is signalled in chapter 3, verses 14 to 24, especially in the reference to banishment from the presence of God in the garden.

What follows in chapters 4 to 11 illustrates the negative side of Exodus 34, verses 6 to 7: one generation's misdemeanours often have significant repercussions on subsequent generations. Patterns of self-centredness that emerged between the first husband and wife were clearly observed and copied by their children. By the time whole nations emerged in Genesis 6, made up of families, clans and tribes, the potential for destruction and perversion had reached mammoth proportions and called for an equally horrendous divine response — the flood.

Community-forming and work

Genesis 4 moves beyond a focus on an *individual* response to God and creation — Adam and Eve — to the social and cultural outworkings of life outside Eden — Cain and Abel. Two clear themes merge here, as the writer of the primeval story prepares the reader for patriarchal history, from chapter 12 onwards. First, the building of community outside of Eden will inevitably have a destructive and violent element to it if God does not energise it. Second, culture and civilisation evolve because of the progressive division of labour that flows out of the second mandate, the instruction by God to manage the creation.

Work lies at the very heart of God's plan. Work is the means by which humans maintain and control his good creation, but if it doesn't occur within a harmonious community, chaos will return. If the two cultural tasks of community-building and work are carried out without reference to God, then much of the thought and energy directed to these will be wasted or, at worst, channelled towards destructive enterprises.

Almost half of the rest of Genesis 1 to 11 consists of genealogical tables which link the 'pre-historical' period to patriarchal/global history.[1] These are not merely pieces of quaint social history. There is a theological point to these lists — that the God who creates the world is also the One who guides and governs human history and culture. He calls all of creation to account, setting boundaries for all material and human existence.[2]

Genealogies in other parts of the ancient world started with the birth of the gods and moved on to the birth of kings; they were set above the historical. Westermann says they grew out of earlier narratives, becoming more formalised over time via lists. He draws attention to five different functions of genealogies in the biblical material:

(a) explaining the meaning of names (for example, chapter 4, verse 1b);
(b) conveying information about professions and crafts (for example, chapter 4, verses 17 to 22);
(c) describing the spread of humankind over the earth (for example, chapter 10, verse 18b);
(d) moving the primeval story onto the stage of world history, geography and politics (for example, chapter 10, verses 10 to 12);
(e) listing sayings of or about people in the genealogies (for example, Nimrod, chapter 10, verse 9b);

   An isolated case occurs in chapter 4, verse 26, where the beginning of the cult is included in the story of beginnings.[3]

The birth of Cain and the shaping of social order (chapter 4, verses 1 and 2)

The Hebrew verb 'to know' often refers to the intimacy of sexual intercourse. The old legal charge of carnal 'knowledge' — having sex with a minor — comes from this meaning. It was used of God's election of his own people in Genesis 18, verse 19.

The word 'knowledge' doesn't have the modern sense of processing information or awareness of some fact or truth, which goes back to Greek philosophical categories of thought.

'I have created a man [together] with *Yahweh*' is the woman's cry of triumph and exhilaration at the experience of childbirth. This allows her to play a major role in carrying out the first of the two cultural mandates, forming community. The Hebrew verb *qanah* generally means 'to acquire, to purchase', but can also mean 'to create', from its Ugaritic root.[4]

Eve's excitement stems from the sense of partnership in creation she has with God. Childbirth is often a religious experience that takes a woman through her own pain into the transcendent world. There are similar illustrations from other cases of human creativity, such as art, music, dance, drama, pottery and gardening.

When Abel became the sheep breeder and Cain the tiller of the ground, community began to take shape. The second mandate, managing the creation, comes into focus through this division of labour. There is no judgment here on the relative value of one occupation over against the other, even though Cain's offering fails to meet with God's approval. Civilisation can only develop through the division of labour.

If humans take up the challenge of forming community and managing the creation, diverse gifts must be channelled into economically productive activity. There will, however, be a need for social and political structures that protect the weak and the poor from exploitation — a result of ejection from Eden and the presence, protection and governance of the Lord God.

Abel's name means 'breath, nothingness' and, when linked to his own fate and to the earlier description of humanity as 'dust', reinforces the essential contingency and fragility of human life.

The sacrifice and God's response to it (chapter 4, verses 3 to 7)

Religious sacrifice was common to most ancient cultures and was linked to their economic survival — the fertility of womb and land, air and sea. From earliest times, people have been aware of their dependence on forces beyond themselves for daily subsistence, especially in an era of hunting, fishing and food-gathering. The practices as mentioned here represented an acknowledgment of divine providence and gratitude for one's 'daily bread'.

While many contemporary thinkers see economics as a value-free activity unfettered by issues of morality, the writer of Genesis underlines the sacred character of all economic activity. It is God the creator who endows the earth with the ongoing capacity to reproduce and thus provide humans and all animal life with daily sustenance (Genesis 1, verses 11 to 25).

Thankfulness and indebtedness may well lie at the heart of all religious behaviour and worship. The notion of 'first fruits' and 'tithes', developed under Israelite law, flows naturally out of this theological principle. The founding fathers of America certainly had this in mind when instituting Thanksgiving Day.

The point of such sacrifices is that work is never seen as an end in itself or even as a means to personal or social advancement; but rather as a form of partnership with God in carrying on his ultimate work of deriving enjoyment and blessing from the ordering of his creation. It is worth noting, along with Paul in Romans 12, verses 1 to 2, that worship is essentially an offering of all that makes us human, including our work and companionship, in gratitude and service at the divine altar.

God responds very differently to the sacrifices of Cain and Abel. Some have tried to explain the difference as a difference in *quality*: Abel gave the best part to God and Cain the mere minimum. Others from a Reformed tradition speak of the election of Abel and rejection of Cain. The text gives no support for the former and only indirect support for the latter interpretation.

The writer offers no explanation and assumes that if God appears to act somewhat arbitrarily, then humans have no choice but to accept such decisions.

We're not told how the two sacrifices were offered — on altars, burnt, or laid out on the ground — or how Cain knew his own offering was rejected. Such considerations were not central to the writer's purpose.

The focus is on how Cain deals with disappointment or rejection — especially when God seems instrumental in it. Life outside of Eden serves up many inequalities — sibling rivalries with roots in jealousy; or being bypassed for a promotion at work. What matters is how people react to apparently arbitrary forces, both positive and negative.

Cain's reaction to God's preference for his younger brother's sacrifice is excessive and totally irrational. Cain was so angry that he cut himself off from all communication. 'His countenance fell' signifies that he wasn't even prepared to look Abel in the eye!

Certainly he had reason to be angry, but where he comes unstuck is in allowing his jealousy to disrupt and destroy familial relationships — initially, by cutting off communication with a brother. Such bonds are a gift from God and form the basis of personal and social well-being. The family unit that functions as God intends provides the solidarity that enables us to cope with the knocks. The writer shows how human emotions, if uncontrolled, can do devastating damage to such primary social units.

In Genesis 3, verse 9, God calls Adam to account

after the fruit is eaten, offering him a chance to own his actions, repent and make a fresh start. Here God engages Cain *before* the murder and while his rage burns. The question, 'Why are you angry and downcast?' invites Cain to identify what's going on inside — a well-known counselling device. Many emotional problems would be resolved if the victims felt they had a forum for talking them through — which is why the intimacy and community outlined in Genesis 2, verse 18 are central to God's plan for all humans.

God warns Cain that he must gain mastery over his emotions and will; if not, he will be overwhelmed by evil forces which lurk at his doorstep. God asks Cain for serious self-examination: if Cain's actions are proper, then there's nothing to be ashamed of or feel guilty about. The onus is on him to behave well and be vigilant.

The murder and its individual and social consequences (verses 8 to 16)

The murder is described in a brief and matter-of-fact way. The horror of Cain's action lies in the fact that he has just offered a sacrifice to God. Being human includes being capable of contradictory behaviour, particularly when freed from the fear of detection — one famous biblical example being David's victories over the Philistines, then his adultery and murder during R & R. Some of us find it hard to accept reality — however unfair it may seem — and try to change it or seek compensation for a perceived disadvantage. Others, like Cain, turn to violence, scapegoating — (though Cain should have blamed God, not his brother!) and revenge.

As in chapter 3, God acts directly as judge and blood avenger, whereas all other legal disputes in the Old Testament are tried by Israel's judicial leaders.[5] God's question 'Where is your brother Abel?' echoes the question to Adam in chapter 3, 'Where are you?' Both questions signal the clear line of accountability — whether they acknowledge it or not — between humans and the divine creator and judge.

There are two areas of human responsibility: first, the need to exercise our own identity in relation to God — fellowship means blessing and alienation means judgment; and second, the need to take up our responsibility for communal well-being and solidarity.

Outside of God as a reference point, humans will always get a distorted view of themselves and of their place in society. Such a world view will inevitably lead to futile or even destructive behaviour — a point made in Romans 1, verses 18 to 32. Psychology and other caring professions can help damaged people find meaning at a human level. Theologically, however, only God as the ultimate helper and meaning-giver can bring wholeness and purpose to life.

Cain's response is the cynical tactic of the self-interested and apathetic of any age in the face of suffering, poverty, famine or violence. It represents the refusal to see oneself potentially as the sufferer who might need help one day. It is the arrogant taunt of those who blame the victim ('They got themselves into this mess, so they should get themselves out of it!'). 'Am I to shepherd the shepherd?' (verse 9) is the thought behind Cain's cynical response to God's question — that is, after his blatant lie.

God's implicit response is that brothers ought to 'stick' to each other in the same way that husbands ought to protect and be loyal to their wives (chapter 2, verse 24). Righteousness in primary relationships is the foundation of all social well-being. The skills of community-building — of serving others and of putting their needs ahead of our wants — must first be learned and practised within each of our own families, before they carry any force at a wider level.

'Your brother's blood is crying to me from the ground' (verse 10) comes as the high point of the narrative, according to Westermann.[6] Cain thinks that the business of Abel concludes with his murder: get rid of the perceived problem and life will be better! Tragically our perceptions, like Cain's, can be distorted by other factors — disease, depression, abuse, indoctrination or stubborn self-will. Abel wasn't Cain's main problem; he was merely the presenting symptom. Jealousy and discontent were the real problems.

God makes it clear that violence of this sort cannot be simply buried under the ground. Even if the life of another human being has been eliminated or the voice of a prophet silenced by the guns of a death squad, God as author of life and judge of all flesh hears the cry of the victim. If no-one else grieves over war, crime, famine, earthquake, disease or accident, there is One whose heart aches. If no-one else is prepared to call those responsible to account, God demands satisfaction and retribution.

Even the ground on which Cain, the tiller of soil, works for his living will, according to chapter 4, verse 12, protest at such 'pollution' by denying him any fruit — by fertility and productivity — for his labour. There is a definite link established here between morality and economic productivity.

God's curse falls in two fundamental ways on Cain: first, his productivity and economic rewards will be severely curtailed (verse 12); second, he is to be ostracised — made taboo — from his own community and forced into a nomadic and rootless existence — to be hunted and hounded for life.

Cain must bear the full weight of his sin-alienation from God, community and soil (verse 14). He must hide from God's wrath which threatens to destroy him. Anxiety and fear will dominate his world. The fact that verse 14 presupposes the existence of other humans — Cain's avenger and his wife — needn't concern us if we remember we are dealing with primeval, not historical events.

Despite the curse, there is divine protection for Cain through a mark (verse 15), which warns people against harming him. There has been speculation as to the form of the mark: tattoo, incision on the face, peculiar hairstyle, circumcision — even a dog as a companion![7] We must allow the intention of the author to guide us: all that can be said is that such a question was not as important to the author as the fact that God *cared enough* for a murderer to provide physical protection — almost like the covering of skins in Genesis 3, verse 21. 'Nod', verse 16, is not a geographical reference, but confirmation of the type of wandering to which Cain was banished. 'East of Eden', likewise, refers to a state of alienation from God.

Genealogical data and God's purposes (chapter 4, verse 17 to chapter 5, verse 26)

Here there are two genealogical tables, one following from Cain and the other from Seth. Both indicate something of God's purposes for society.

First, with regard to the Cainite genealogy, commentators tend to infer — through the link between the genealogy of Cain and the growth of urbanisation, nomadism, music and metallurgy — that 'all aspects of human culture are in some way tainted by Cain's sin'.[8] A fairer assessment is that, outside of Eden, social, technological and cultural development bring with them the potential for good and evil. God's cultural mandate to humankind remains the same — to build community and manage God's now flawed world.

There are interesting parallels with Sumerian texts. Seven *apkallu*, 'wise ones', taught the various aspects of civilisation before the flood. The first sage, Adapa, 'rose from the sea and taught man the arts of writing, agriculture and city-building'.[9] Another was apparently inventor of the lyre.[10]

❑ *The family of Cain*

The first section of the Cainite genealogy (chapter 4, verses 17 and 18) covers seven generations: Adam, Cain, Enoch, Irad, Mehujael, Methushael and Lamech. The second part (verses 19 to 24), shows how through one generation (Lamech's), different lifestyles are established. The growth of both sedentary and nomadic lifestyles reflects Israel's story of wanderings, settlement and exile. Deuteronomy 26, verses 5 to 9 gives a picture of this aspect of Israel's life.

The names in the Cainite genealogical table seem to say something of Hebrew origins, preoccupations and society. It is almost impossible to explain their meaning; they are not Hebrew, but possibly

Babylonian. 'Irad' may be a form of 'Eridu', tradi-
tionally the oldest Mesopotamian city. 'Mehujael'
could mean 'God strikes and gives life' or 'God's
priest, seer'. 'Methushael' may mean 'man of God',
'man of the underworld' or 'man of desire, man of
prayer'. 'Lamech' is usually sourced to the
Sumerian 'lumga', the title of the sky god *Ea*, patron
of music; otherwise it is derived from an Akkadian
word meaning 'class of priests', or an Arabic word
meaning 'strong youths or oppressor'.

'Adah' is possibly linked to a word meaning
'ornament'; 'Zillah' to words meaning 'shade' or
'cymbal'. The names of Lamech's children derive
from the Hebrew word meaning 'product'. 'Tubal'
is Hebrew for the smith or artificer.

The reference to iron in verse 22 may seem
anachronistic, since iron was first smelted only in
the second millennium BC. The development of
metallurgy was regarded as of central importance to
the growth of civilisation; such a reference therefore
is more likely to represent the author's attempt to
link primeval history with later urbanising forces,
the iron being of symbolic significance.

Having been responsible for founding specific
cultural and technological enterprises, Adah and Zillah now listen with horror to the vengeful boasting
of their husband, Lamech (verses 23 and 24). Life
outside Eden brings with it the potential for
creativity through the growth of the arts and tech-

nology, but also, tragically, the danger of violence and terror from within the very same family.

❏ The family of Seth

We now turn to the second, the Seth genealogy (Genesis 4, verse 25 to chapter 5, verse 32). The gospel in the Old Testament is that new beginnings are part of God's gracious way of healing the hurts of our past. Cain as the firstborn son of Adam and Eve failed to fulfil the twofold mandate. The community resulting from his family line was culturally innovative but socially destructive. God grants Eve another son, Seth, in place of the murdered Abel and begins to unfold his plan of restoration and reconciliation.

Seth's son and father both have the same meaning for their names — Adam and Enosh, which mean 'man'. God's new beginning is to unfold through the genealogical line of the 'new man'. This passage affirms, D.J.A. Clines says, that 'the world of men is not totally given over to the Cainite lifestyle. Even while the race of Cain is increasing in congenital violence. . . elsewhere there is a line of men who have begun to "call on the name of Yahweh".'[11] In the genealogy in Luke 3, verses 23 to 38, Christ is the exact fulfilment of such ideas in his role as the 'second Adam'.

The most significant fact about the life and times of Enosh was that people 'began to invoke the name of Yahweh' (verse 26). A problem here is that Exodus 6, verses 2 to 3 and Exodus 3, verse 15 make this reference to the name 'Yahweh' seem anachronistic. One way around the problem is to read it back into an earlier period without the connotations it had for Israel as Yahweh's covenant community. In other words, the universal practice of religion and cultic observance has its origins in the days of Enosh. The name 'Yahu/weh' may have been used in the Semitic language before being incorporated into Israelite religion.

Calling on God's name via prayer and sacrifice is set alongside, not separate from other human enterprises such as agriculture, the arts, urbanisation and metallurgy. It is normal to invoke God's protection and blessing for the whole of life, rather than compartmentalising it into sacred and secular domains. Contemporary forms of Christianity — worship, preaching, education and management structures — can reinforce this dualism and rob the gospel of much of its social power and cultural relevance.

The words in chapter 5, verse 1, 'This is the list of the descendants of Adam', suggests that the writer is referring to an actual document consisting of several lists of genealogies. No reasonable explanation of the length of the lives of people in these lists has yet been found, nor of the discrepancies between such Old Testament texts as the Masoretic Text,

Samaritan Pentateuch and LXX numberings.[12]

The primary social unit in the ancient world was the tribe or family. Whole meaning systems depended on the sense of one's familial roots, which had to be verifiable. The reader might be inclined to 'fast-forward' such scriptures as irrelevant. The real force of such literature lies in the message that human existence is marked by this 'steady, ongoing rhythm of events. . . birth, length of life, begetting, death'.[13] The genealogies remind us of the power of God's original blessing on the first humans to 'be fruitful and multiply'. Yet the corrective to human pride lies in the monotonous cycle which always terminates in death.

In Genesis 5, verse 2, there is the repetition of statements about the uniqueness of humans as the pinnacle of creation, but also a new description — 'they were created "humankind"' — for which the word 'Adam' is used. Adam's children are then described in verse 3, significantly, as 'in his likeness, according to his image'. The image of God with which Adam was stamped was automatically transferred to his children, despite the effects of the fall. Chapter 4, verse 25 seems to contradict chapter 5, verse 3 as far as who actually named Seth, the normal custom being for the man to do the naming.

Again, in this Seth genealogy, the names indicate Hebrew associations and preoccupations. 'Kenan' (verse 12) is a variant of Cain and was the name of a Sabean god; 'Mahalel' (verse 12) means 'one who praises God, the praise of God'. 'Jared' (verse 15) possibly means 'go down', though it might come from an Akkadian word meaning 'servant'. 'Enoch' (verse 21) probably means 'dedicated'; 'Methuselah' means man of Shelah; Noah means 'comfort, rest'; 'Shem' means 'name'; 'Ham' means 'hot' (from 'Hammu', a West Semitic sun-god); 'Japheth' possibly means 'May [Yahweh] enlarge [him]'.

'And he fathered sons and daughters' is a clause that occurs nine times throughout the list. The interest, of course, is in the male line, since that was how the Semitic world view defined reality.

Enoch comes in for special commendation: 'Enoch walked with God and he was not, for God took him' (verse 24). Enoch lived for 365 years — a symbol of fullness and totality. More important than quantity was the quality of his life. Only Enoch and Noah are said to have walked 'with God'. They stood in some unique relationship with God — as Gordon Wenham says, they had 'a special intimacy with God and a life of piety'.[14] Once again, the idea of fellowship with God as a 'walk' comes through.

The only explanation for Enoch's disappearance was a theological one — 'God took him'. Unlike all others in the family history — they 'died' — Enoch is given special status by being taken by God.

Noah is a central figure in God's plan to save his creation. The prophecy associated with his birth

(Genesis 5, verse 29), points to the impending flood, through which God's judgment on humanity and the creation of a community with whom he develops a covenant, take place. Relief will come after the flawed and rebellious creation is purged.

The theological link between creation and redemption commences with Noah, with the reference to relief for the cursed soil on the one hand, and to the genealogical link from Noah's son, Shem (chapter 5, verse 32) to the first of the patriarchs, Abraham (chapter 11, verses 10 to 32), on the other. The fate of the whole human enterprise, defined by God's twofold mandate, hinges on Noah and his progeny.

The rest, relief and comfort that God graciously provides through Noah's seed will only be fully realised in the saving work of Jesus Christ. For now, however, the writer makes the link between the effects of sin on work (chapter 5, verse 29).

Discussion questions

Talking it through

1 Cain killed Abel — the first murder in human society *and* within the family! What can we learn from the Cain-Abel story about:
* God's character?
* primitive religion?
* human nature?
* ethics and social responsibility?
* the social consequences of sin?

2 What does the offering of sacrifice (verses 3 and 4) and 'calling on the name of the Lord' (verse 26) tell us about primitive religion? Were Cain and Abel trying to placate an angry God?

3 What does the Lamech story (chapter 4, verses 18 to 24) teach us about how culture and society become complex? Why, do you think, does this story even feature in the Bible?

4 'Skip the genealogical tables — they're boring and irrelevant.' Why is such a view of Genesis 5 misguided? What do these lists of names tell us:
(a) about God?
(b) about God's people?

5 What did it mean in Enoch's day to 'walk with God' (chapter 5, verse 22)? What does it mean today?

Widening our horizons

1 'With the help of the Lord I have brought into being a male child' (chapter 4, verse 1). Such a religious perspective on sexual reproduction has largely been supplanted by medical technology and a mechanistic world view. Childbirth in modern societies is much safer, but its mystery has been removed.

What difference can awe and thankfulness make to our view of childbirth? How can we help others to have such a view?

2 Sibling rivalry is a serious problem in many families. What are some of its causes? Is it inevitable? How might it be resolved?

3 'Am I my brother's keeper?' Using these words as a starting point, how have the social, moral and political demands of the Judaeo-Christian religion been neglected by the contemporary church? Why has this happened and how can it be remedied?

4 The origins of agriculture, music and metallurgy (chapter 4, verses 20 to 22) are
attributed to an evil ancestor. To what extent are cultural and economic activities
intrinsically good or evil? How have such activities been socially beneficial throughout the
ages? What can be done to save these activities from destructive effects?

5 Reproducing things or people in our own
image seems to reflect a deep human need
for meaning and fulfilment, but can be
idolatrous and egotistical.

How do you view the replication of your-
self in your children? Is it a source of pride?
Satisfaction? Meaning? Sheer joy? Foreboding?

Do we get any clue how God views the
creation of beings 'in his own image'? What
can we learn from our thinking about all
this?

4
A drastic reordering of society

What is the significance of the flood?
GENESIS CHAPTER 6, VERSE 1 TO
CHAPTER 9, VERSE 29

SO FAR, WE HAVE SEEN HOW SIN manifests itself in human society and within the creation itself. But there are other ways in which sin can take hold.

Prelude to the flood
(chapter 6, verses 1 to 4)
Here we see sin taking hold in the area of love and sexual union. In Genesis 3, 4 and 11, God intervened when boundaries were transgressed so as to prevent chaos overwhelming humanity. Here God intervenes because heavenly beings overstep the bounds.

We have noticed how male-orientated the genealogical tables are. We now focus on the 'daughters' mentioned in the words, 'he fathered sons and daughters'. Women had little power over their bodies and destinies in a world where men 'saw' them as objects of pleasure and beauty, and 'took' as many of them as they fancied.

As humanity expands outside Eden, the potential increases for the abuse and oppression of women by men who use power — whether political, sexual or socio-economic — to gain advantage over the less powerful, along the lines suggested in chapter 3, verses 1 to 6. 'Sons of' in verse 2, according to Brevard Childs, refers to membership within a guild, society or class of gods.[1] Because they were vastly more powerful than any human, they were able to pick and choose any woman they fancied. Their offspring were demi-gods whose existence, Ronald Hendel says, threatened 'the fabric of the cosmos'.[2]

Three explanations have been offered of the enigmatic phrase 'sons of God/the gods': first (this is not held seriously today), godly humans like Seth and Enoch were intended by the phrase; second, godlike beings such as angels, demons or spirits were intended — in Ugaritic mythology, they were members of the divine pantheon;[3] third, superior men such as kings or famous warriors were meant. Clines suggests they were 'dynastic rulers' who were also semi-divine beings — 'like Gilgamesh, two-thirds god and one-third human'.[4]

There is a strong background of worldly deities in Middle Eastern ancient writings. In Job 1 and 2, Satan is referred to as one of the 'sons of God' in the heavenly court who served God. The Canaanite gods are represented as enjoying sexual intercourse and our author had no problems with the same possibility here. Wenham adds, 'If the modern reader finds this story incredible, that reflects a materialism that tends to doubt the existence of spirits, good or ill. But those who believe that the creator could unite himself to human nature in the Virgin's womb will not find this story. . . beyond belief.'[5]

There may be a reference to the Canaanite fertility cult, through which priests representing the gods had sexual intercourse with virgins just prior to their weddings — a practice intended to secure fertility in marriage, but condemned under Israelite law. Not only did the godlike beings overstep the boundaries in this behaviour, but also in the uncontrolled way they fed their sexual desires by taking 'as many as they fancied'. Both the daughters and their fathers were equally condemned for giving permission to such marriages.

The first eleven chapters of Genesis portray God as intimately involved in the promotion and policing of his twofold mandate. Where people transgress existing boundaries, he intervenes for the sake of order. In verse 3, he imposes limits on the length of life. Childs suggests that the sons of gods may have intermarried with humans to overcome the restriction and find ways of extending human life.[6]

The reference to God's spirit abiding in verse 3 refers to the breath of life that energises humans and is extinguished at death; such energy will not remain for ever, since humans are mortal. Whereas the earliest humans lived for several hundred years, their lifespan is reduced to 120 years, though Abraham (175 years), Isaac (180 years) and Jacob (147 years) lived somewhat beyond this. Attempts by humans to elevate themselves above their station are clearly rejected in the Bible — Isaiah 14, verses 14 and 15 being one example.

The 'Nephilim' were the giants of Numbers 13, verse 33. The word 'naphal' means 'fall'. The link between the sons of gods and the giants is not clear. They were probably 'mythical semi-divine beings', as Westermann says,[7] with unusual progeny from such unions. There is a reference in Ezekiel 32, verse 27 to heroes — *'gibbor'* — who fell down to Sheol fully armed, after having terrorised the world of the living.

God's decision (chapter 6, verses 5 to 21)

We have already noticed how God, reflecting on his work of creation, was able to affirm all he had made. In chapter 1, verse 31, 'God *saw* everything that he had made, and indeed, it was very good.'

In this later section, a different kind of 'performance

appraisal' occurs, with disastrous consequences for the primeval world. In chapter 6, verses 5 and 6, God 'saw. . . was sorry. . . and grieved at heart'. The writer communicates the intense reaction of a holy creator to evil when it is allowed free rein in his world. The source of the problem is clearly in the thoughts and plans of the human mind. (The word 'heart' in verse 5, as in all the Old Testament, is seen as the seat of understanding, will and emotion.[8])

The writer's problem is how to reconcile the divine decision to create, then destroy humanity. The only explanation of such a contradiction is that evil had corrupted humanity across an entire generation or more. Perhaps the arrogance and immorality of the preceding story indicates an increasing defection of humans from God, as well as the growth in violence through the influence of warriors like Lamech and the giants.

Little evidence is given for the profound change within God's mind about his creation. Moral or religious perversion on a massive social scale may lie behind the decision to obliterate humans, animals, birds and creeping things. There is a natural tendency in all cultures to look for religious or moral explanations for natural disasters such as floods, famines, earthquakes and fires. Blaming the victim is common. Jesus in Luke 13, verse 4 refused to make such a direct causal link, but urged repentance on all.

The word 'wickedness' in verse 5 refers to a state,

not an act — the 'planning and devising' underlying all human action. Every human plan and intention is biased towards what is perverse. Such a view of humanity flies in the face of many religions, philosophies and educational and welfare programs.

The Bible's teaching is that when God's authority and wisdom are supplanted, social structures disintegrate. We think we know best how to build community and manage 'our' world. The fact that God's heart was grieved reminds us of the pain within the Godhead at the havoc caused by this perversity. We can trivialise our greed, pride or anger by forgetting the pain and grief inflicted on the heart of a holy God in the death of his Son.

Several questions arise: Why haven't other decadent societies received similar punishment? Where does racism or famine fit? Is John Calvin's notion of total depravity correct? Which of the two basic views of human nature — the pessimistic one (that we are self-centred) and the optimistic one (that we are well-meaning) — has dominated patterns of counselling and social welfare, education, politics, child-rearing and law enforcement over time?

The decision in verse 7 to 'blot out' humankind is based on the bitter disappointment of the creator at the spectacle of the pinnacle of his work being perverted. The utter horror of the divine decision is reflected in the additional clause '. . .The human beings I have created.'

'But Noah found favour in the sight of the Lord,' signals a new beginning, hints of which are given in chapter 3, verse 20 and chapter 5, verse 29. There is one exception to God's condemnation of humanity in verse 5. Noah is singled out by God's grace not Noah's piety (verse 8); though verse 9 refers to Noah's exceptional quality of character.

'Righteous' means loyalty within defined social relationships and legal obligations; 'blameless' referred to the cultic purity or sacrificial wholeness of an unblemished animal. By contrast with his contemporaries, Noah stood out as an example of integrity. The reason for such a life is given as his 'walk' with God. Violence had reached such proportions that, according to verse 11 onwards, the earth had been corrupted. God reviewed creation and saw that 'the earth was corrupt'. The picture is of a God concerned about how his creation develops, not of a distant figure.

God's words in verse 13 are: 'I have determined to make an end of all flesh.' The reason for the flood, von Rad says, is the 'violent breach of a just order'.[9] Such language foreshadows the later apocalyptic literature and serves as a reminder that God holds his creation to account for the way it carries out his mandates to build community and manage creation. Judgment is the inevitable result of human rejection of his authority.

Next, in verse 14, follows the instruction to build

an ark — literally a chest — out of resinous wood (probably cypress), with rooms inside, covered inside and out with pitch. It is to be 300 cubits long, 50 wide and 30 high. A cubit is 444.5 millimetres, so the whole was to be 132 metres by 22 metres by 12 metres. There was to be a door at the side and three decks. Details about the building of the ark — in both Genesis 6 and the *Gilgamesh Epic* — are taken from a common literary source.[10] The roof may have doubled as a skylight.

Noah is to carry out God's instructions for building an ark, and God will bring a 'flood of waters' (verse 17), a reference to the heavenly ocean. The phrase, 'breath of life' (verse 17 — a reference to Genesis 2, verse 7), reminds the reader that the creator has now become the destroyer of life: every living thing on earth is to die.

We also see God's overall purpose in these words from verse 18: 'But I will establish my covenant with you.' God's word of command to Noah and his household is the means of escape and of future blessing. That is what 'covenant' means here: in the face of judgment, God's command is the means of salvation, initially to one family, but over time to all who respond faithfully to the divine command or promise.

Noah is instructed in verses 19 and 20 to take a pair of every existing animal, male and female, into the ark for the purpose of continuing the life cycle.

The writer is not interested in how Noah got, fitted and fed all these animals in the ark; he is asserting that animals and humans alike come under the judgment and saving plan of God. Noah's response was one of unquestioning obedience — 'he did all that God commanded him' (verse 22), a point underlined in Hebrews 11, verse 7.

From chapter 7, verses 1 to 5, God elaborates on the instructions to Noah, drawing a distinction between clean animals (seven pairs) and unclean (two pairs) — the former being more useful in the new order. Such a distinction, which seems to have been universal at this stage, is developed in later Mosaic traditions (see Leviticus 11 and Deuteronomy 14).

Only Noah is seen by God as 'righteous' out of his whole generation (chapter 7, verse 1). It is pointless reading back into this text any Pauline discussion of righteousness, such as Romans 4, verses 1 to 5 or Philippians 2, verses 12 and 13. God judged that the qualities of piety, loyalty to given relationships and morality found in Noah were the building blocks of a new redemptive order to be established.

In verse 4, God announced that the deluge would begin in seven days' time and its duration would be 'forty days and forty nights'. 'Forty' is used at significant points in the Bible. Jesus' temptation was forty days and the children of Israel were forty years in the wilderness.

Flood and destruction
(chapter 7, verses 6 to 24)

We are told that the flood began when Noah was 600 years old; but it is impossible to date it accurately.[11] Verses 7 to 9 indicate the flood forced Noah and his family into the ark, along with the prescribed number of clean and unclean animals, birds and creeping things. The storyteller obviously shared none of the Hollywood scriptwriter's attraction for sensationalism — for a contrast, see Matthew 24, verse 38! There is no reference to those who perished — only to those who were saved.

Verse 11 says, 'All the fountains of the great deep burst forth, and the windows of the heavens were opened.' The same imagery is used of the dividing of the Reed Sea in Exodus 14, verse 16. Chaos returns when the windows of heaven are opened, allowing the subterranean waters to meet the waters above the 'firmament vault' and cause devastating floods on earth. There was nothing to stop the flow once the verdict had been handed down. The effects took on, as Westermann says, 'supranatural, mythical-cosmic' proportions.[12]

Only our imagination can tell us what might have been going on in the minds of Noah's family as they entered the ark. The author wants us to note, however, the matter-of-factness about the response of faith in obedience to the command of God. The amazing procession of animals of every kind in pairs

— no reference to 'sevens' here — is described in verses 15 and 16 as being 'with Noah. . . as God had commanded him'.

In coming to Noah in the ark, the ark's cargo found salvation, in much the same way, in New Testament thought, as all who come to Jesus. Jesus, from Noah's line of descendants, was to escape condemnation and find life. Noah was to act in obedience to and under the authority of the creator and judge of all things — on earth, under the sea and in the heavens — just as the perfect Son of God was at all times, in his ministry on earth, under his Father's authority — a point made in John 15, verse 10.

In the *Gilgamesh Epic*, Noah's equivalent, Utnapishtim, closes the entrance from within the ark, whereas here God 'shut him in' (verse 16), highlighting the comprehensiveness of God's role in carrying out his covenant.

In chapter 1, verse 2, we noted how the storm wind/breath of God — *'ruach elohim'* — was hovering 'over the surface of the waters', while the darkness was 'over the surface of the deep'. There, the threat of chaos overwhelming the cosmos was negated only by God's command ('let there be. . .') that divided alien and destructive forces and ordered the chaos. Here chaos has overwhelmed the created order as a result of God's word of judgment upon human depravity. This time the ark floats 'on the face of the waters', bringing new life in the face of mass destruction.

All living flesh perished: animals, birds, reptiles and humans. The cause of such destruction is simply noted in verse 23: 'He blotted out every living thing that was on the face of the ground.' Because of the problem of attributing evil to God, some translations opt for a passive reading of the verb 'blot out'. The New Jerusalem Bible says, 'Every living thing. . . was wiped out.' The problem of evil — of God appearing to do more than allow nature to take its course — remains a stumbling block to faith today.

But God's action is not quite as grim as the first part of verse 23 suggests. The verse goes on to say, 'Only Noah was left, and those that were with him in the ark.' Here is the concept of 'the remnant', a divine mechanism for ensuring that the purposes of God are preserved through a righteous line. God's sovereign purposes after Genesis 3 are preserved through Seth, Noah, Shem, Abraham, Joseph, David and Christ. After the fall, the masses turn aside from a God-centred orientation, with death and retribution the outcome; only a few pursue righteousness and faith, with long life and blessing the outcome.

God's purpose for the redemption of the cosmos has always depended on a faithful few in each generation.

The new world order
(chapter 8, verses 1 to 22)

Bernhard Anderson shows how the structure of the
flood narrative is balanced around the movement
towards chaos in the first part (chapter 7) and
towards the new creation in the second (chapter 8).[13]
While the flood does its destructive work, God's
purposes for his creation have not been abandoned.
He 'remembered Noah', he had Noah in mind —
and all animals in the ark with him (chapter 8, verse
1).

The same verb for 'remembering' is used in Exodus 2, verse 24 to refer to God's calling to mind
of his covenant with Abraham, Isaac and Jacob,
when the Israelites are languishing under the op-
pressive yoke of Egyptian slavery. The same idea
is in Genesis 19, verse 29, where God 'remembered
Abraham'. The force of the verb lies in both the
crises confronting those in the ark and also in the
elective purpose of God to start afresh through
Noah's line: God is both creator and rescuer.

It is through the action of wind that God's
deliverance is effected on behalf of his covenant
community. At the same time, the 'fountains of the
deep and the windows of the heavens were closed'
and the downpour from the skies checked (verse 2).

After 150 days, the waters abated and the ark
came to rest on 'the mountains of Ararat', which
represented, Gerhard von Rad says, the highest

mountain in the known world.[14] Ararat is described
in 2 Kings 19, verse 37, as a 'land' and in Jeremiah
51, verse 27 as a 'kingdom'. In Akkadian, it refers
to mountain country to the west of the Tigris.[15]
Perhaps it was a place of refuge in a mountainous
region whose exact location is unclear to this day.

Three attempts were made by Noah to take water
level soundings before disembarking. The aim was
to 'see' (verse 8) if the waters had yet abated. How
did Noah learn such techniques for using birds in
this way? Von Rad says mariners often used birds
this way in the ancient world. The fact that Noah
knew of the practice only highlights the wisdom of
one 'who knew what to do in such pressing
circumstances'.[16] Initially a crow — 'a raven' (verse
7) — flew to and fro. Next a dove was sent out,
but it found no resting place (verse 9). Its welcome
by Noah is described movingly in verse 9 and
reminds us of the harmony, security and mutual
trust within the created order: all who come to
Noah — even the birds of the air — will find rest.
The final sorties served as a witness to Noah, who
deduced — literally 'knew' — that relief was im-
minent.

'New Year's Day' was on the day the land dried
up: 601 refers to Noah's age at the time. Verse 13
seems to give a rather different account of the exit
from the ark to the one just offered; it is likely that
two independent narratives are merged by a later

editor. Noah simply lifts back the hatch of the ark and finds dry ground.

The writer reminds us that salvation, like judgment, is governed by God's command: 'Then God said to Noah, "Go out of the ark."' This command both authorises and defines any future reality for Noah's family and for the animals which can breed once again.

The original blessing is renewed in verse 17 — 'abound. . . be fruitful and multiply on the earth'; even in a radically flawed and now vulnerable era, God's command enables life, fertility and community to take place.

Various explanations of Noah's sacrifice in verse 20 have been offered — a sacrifice of reconciliation, an act of appeasement, propitiation and thanksgiving. All seem legitimate, though the response of God in verse 21 possibly indicates appeasement or propitiation — 'I will never again curse the ground because of humankind.' It is worth noting that this sentence comes not as a pronouncement to Noah, but as a reflection by God 'to his heart'. 'God smelled the soothing odour,' states verse 21. God accepted Noah's sacrifice and averted his wrath.

In verse 21, God says: '. . .nor will I ever again destroy every living creature as I have done'. It is somewhat puzzling as to why God chooses to 'change policy' at this point, having blotted out one whole civilisation because of its degeneracy. God cursed the ground in Genesis 3, verse 17 when Adam disobeyed and the result was weeds and thorns — a curse that remains on all of our gardens!

The flood represented the devastation of the earth and of all its inhabitants. For some reason (was it the efficacy of Noah's sacrifice?) God decided not to blot out each successive civilisation — which raises the problem of justice for those obliterated, relative to those let off. From the flood onwards, God was to allow goodness and evil to co-exist in society. The prognosis seems gloomy because of the serious flaw and bias in human nature.

God has decided to maintain order throughout the creation — even when humans go their own way. God was never again to be responsible for the punishment and destruction of life on such a massive scale. There might be periodic natural disasters, but only at a localised level. When such tragedies occur, it is legitimate to assert that the harmony of creation flows out of a gracious decision of God's not to turn creation against us and to call for repentance in the light of the coming judgment of Revelation 21, verse 1 on all creation.

In verse 22, God says, 'As long as the earth endures [various blessings] shall not cease.' Here is an affirmation of both permanence and contingency. While the life of the earth continues, the cycle of creation with its division of seasons will not cease. But the implication is that the days of the earth are numbered. The blessings inherent in such a cycle are those mentioned already — of fertility, productivity and long life. These must never be taken for granted; they are a gift of God's grace and a sign of his patience.

Two views of time occur in Genesis 1 to 11: linear and cyclic time. This verse, on the one hand, sees time as a constantly repeated, monotonously regular series of cycles — summer and winter, planting and harvesting, cold and hot temperatures, day and night. It is the same pattern referred to by the Preacher in Ecclesiastes and in Acts 14, verse 17. There is nothing any of us can do to alter this cycle.

But, on the other hand, there is no need to resort to fatalism, because of the contingency of the earth: 'As long as the earth endures. . .' None of us knows when life on earth will cease — that is God's domain. Our responsibility is to live within the boundaries of his loving provision, to build community and manage creation. The same God who appears to let nature take its course, season after season, is the One who guides cosmic and human history to its intended goal or endpoint. Colossians 1, verses 16 to 20 and 1 Corinthians 15, verse 28 elaborate this point.

Blessing the new world order
(chapter 9, verses 1 to 17)
The blessing at creation is reissued to Noah and his sons, but with an additional note of reality as a result

of the potential in the new order for violence on the earth. What was once an environment adjudged by the creator as 'very good' now has the threat of violence — what von Rad calls 'reciprocal killing' and conflict. Hence the importance of the divine blessing on the new order. We have noted the potential for life and death, for peace and violence. God consigns all living creatures — beasts, birds, creeping things and fish — into human hands, thereby subjecting them to the threat of extermination. Here, as in chapter 3, verse 15 with the serpent's existence after the fall, is a clear description — not prescription — of how things will be as a result of human sin.

Humans are now allowed to eat the flesh of animals. This is in contrast to chapter 1, verses 28 to 30 when God gave not only to the man and the woman, but all the creatures who shared their food supply 'every green plant for food'. All this now changes. Here God assigns 'every moving thing that is alive' as food for human consumption (verse 3). Unlike the later dietary restrictions in Deuteronomy 14, verses 3 to 20, no restrictions about clean or unclean animals, birds or sea life are laid down. Such distinctions result from a dualism that was never intended originally.

The only restriction is on the consumption of animals' blood (chapter 9, verse 4). There doesn't appear to be any suggestion in the Semitic world that blood had some intrinsically divine quality in it. The meaning seems to be that animal flesh can be eaten only after its life-blood has been poured out or separated. Gerhard von Rad says, 'Even when man slaughters and kills, he is to know that he is touching something which, because it is life, is in a special manner God's property; and as a sign of this he is to keep his hands off the blood.'[17] The ultimate taboo is life — with God as its author — symbolised in the blood. Note that there is a linguistic connection between the words 'blood' (*dahm*), 'man' (*adahm*), and 'earth' (*adahmah*).

Anyone who intrudes into God's area of sovereignty over human life will have God as their blood avenger (verse 5). Even animals that kill humans will face the same retribution. Any human who takes the life of another human — literally, 'his brother' — will forfeit his life. Such is the solidarity between members of a community, that nothing — on pain of death — is to threaten the life of that community. The community is responsible for seeing that murderers are punished. The verb *darash* in verse 5, translated as 'require a reckoning', means 'look for, demand account for, revenge'. That is, the blood of the one murdered is to be avenged in the life of the murderer.

Von Rad sees this as a reference to institutionalised law enforcement — what he calls a 'constitutive ordinance'.[18] The reason for the severity of such punishment is given as the fact that humans are made in the image of God and therefore murder is a direct assault on God (verse 6). This point is elaborated in Ezekiel 18, verse 4. It is important to understand theologically why such a prohibition against bloodshed is foundational for a Judaeo-Christian ethic. The value of a human life is so high that whoever dares to take life away, Westermann says, is guilty of 'direct and unbridled revolt against God'.[19] This is a rebuke to the casual way in which modern society treats murder and mayhem.

In the meantime, verse 7 indicates that Noah's family must take up the original challenge to build community: 'be fruitful and multiply, abound on the earth and multiply in it.'

A covenant — berith — in the ancient Near East was a legally binding contract usually between two unequal partners, with mutual obligations that were sealed in some formal way. With the Abrahamic covenant, Abraham circumcised all males in his household and was required to follow God with his family all his days.[20]

With Noah, the commitment is entirely from God's side; it is with Noah and all living things in the post-flood resettlement period; it is of a purely negative kind — 'nor will I ever again destroy every living creature' — and it is sealed by the rainbow, which serves as a reminder to God of the self-obligation he has made. It is interesting that in Isaiah 54, verse 9, the covenant with Noah is described as an oath.

In verse 13, God designates his rainbow in the clouds as a symbol, a reminder of his self-imposed obligation. It may be somewhat speculative, but there is a similarity between the original idea — and possibly even the etymology — of the word 'creation', *bahrah*, as dividing or separating opposites, and 'covenant', *berith*, referring to a sign that divides two opposing spheres — that of a holy God in heaven and that of a sinful people on earth.

The rainbow in the clouds, coming between heaven and earth, represents the rift between God and his people as well as reconciliation between the two spheres. So there is the double purpose of reminding both parties of the covenant of judgment and salvation. If there is a rift or even hostility between God and his creation, then the rainbow graphically illustrates it, while at the same time pointing to a gracious means of reconciliation between the conflicting parties.

Whereas God once vented the full force of his wrath on Noah's generation, he now pledges, as he did at creation, that the earth is under his protection. Despite appearances to the contrary (the darkness and foreboding of a storm cloud), the gospel according to Noah is that God offers light — the very nature of the rainbow! — hope and peace to all who take heed of the message represented in the rainbow.

He undertakes to mind his promise and 'remember the everlasting covenant' between God and every living creature'.[21]

Whether the flood story is to be taken as a universal or partial flood depends on what the writer or editor meant by phrases such as 'all the earth', 'the [dry] land', 'from the earth', 'every living thing'. It probably makes most sense to take these phrases to mean the known world which was, Westermann says, a 'flat surface. . . bounded by the areas described in Genesis 10.'[22]

The ordering of the community
(chapter 9, verses 18 to 29)

The 'whole earth' is now described as being populated, literally 'scattered', by the three sons of Noah — presumably, another localised reference to the then-known world of our author. The notion of 'scattering' or 'dispersion' of peoples is taken up pejoratively — as a punishment by God — in Genesis 11, verse 8 onwards and Isaiah 33, verse 3.

Noah took up farming — verse 20 says he was 'a man of the soil' — and was the first to cultivate the vine. Viniculture is one stage beyond primitive agriculture. Its practice by Noah shows how he fulfils the prophecy in Genesis 5, verse 29, about his role in bringing relief from human toil. Naturally, the 'inventor' gets to test the product first, but also to experience its potency! The fruit of the vine was

symbolic in Israelite thought of the fulfilment of
God's covenant blessings of peace, fertility and long
life.[23]

The public nakedness of Noah in verse 21 was a
disgrace in Israel's eyes. Nakedness, as already
noted after the fall, is a private matter. Drunkenness
was known for its association with nakedness in
Israel in places like Habakkuk 2, verse 15 and
Lamentations 4, verse 21.

The writer doesn't condemn Noah for his
drunkenness or nakedness; the point of the story
becomes clearer in the contrasting reactions of his
three sons to the situation. Ham, father of Canaan,
should have known better. Though we're not told
what mistake he made, the reason must be inferred.
The fault seems to have been in gazing upon his
father, so invading his privacy, and then talking
about the nakedness, so drawing attention to it and
making it a point for ridicule.

The Old Testament story about the curse on
Canaan has often been interpreted in the light of the
Israelite conquest of Canaan. For example, it has
been said that the story aims to discredit the
Canaanites and justify the Israelite and Philistine
hegemony over them. Some have speculated about
possible incest, pederasty, even castration.[24]

On the contrary, the writer is highlighting the
importance of filial piety, whereby a son's responsibility is always to protect — to cover the nakedness

of — and respect his father. The life and integrity of the community depends on this fundamental loyalty within a family unit. Shem and Japheth demonstrated their own righteousness by covering their father's nakedness without looking on it in verse 23. This gives point to the subsequent curse.

Von Rad tries to link the passage with the reason for Israel's later rejection of Canaanite religious and moral customs. The focus, however, seems to be on responsibilities of individual members of the primal family, rather than an attempt to justify later events.

Enslavement within families, where brothers subjugate brothers, is pronounced as a curse on Canaan, not Ham. One must ask why Ham isn't cursed directly, for the author seems more interested in the effects of the curse on the son than on the father.

By way of contrast, Shem will be blessed and will have Canaan serving him. Even Japheth is to dwell in Shem's tents (verse 27), which leads Westermann to equate Shem with Israel, 'because Yahweh is the God of Israel only'.[26] The blessing on Japheth in verse 27 seems to be via Shem. Von Rad refers to the fact that Israel was to share occupancy of the land as a 'riddle in God's guidance of history' and to the likelihood that 'Japheth', therefore, meant the Philistines.[27] Westermann, however, infers a location somewhere in Asia Minor, where Japheth's sons are said to be based.[28]

The passing on of tradition

It is worth noting that the author highlights our vulnerability, in the community-building process, in three basic relationships: man-woman in chapter 3, brother-brother in chapter 4 and father-son in chapter 9. As the fourth commandment underlines, the best traditions of any society or culture will only provide stability in subsequent generations, if the younger generation demonstrates a healthy respect for the older. As respect for moral codes, norms or traditions declines, the very fabric of a society disintegrates — a fundamental reason for God's intervention in Noah's generation, but also a major problem for a pluralistic, ethically relativistic society such as ours today.[29]

The relationship between fathers and their sons is important in the Bible: as a means of passing on the values and beliefs of one's culture, and of securing stable and healthy human resources for subsequent generations' efforts to carry out the twofold mandate of creation — management and community building.

The saga of wayward sons in the history of salvation — Adam and Cain; Methuselah and Lamech; Ham and Canaan; Isaac and Esau; Eli and Hophni and Phinehas; Aaron and Nadab and Abihu; and David and Absalom — serves as a salutary warning to fathers today. This is especially when career demands, social obligations or even church commitments — legitimate in themselves perhaps — divert them from the priority of nurturing, guiding and educating their own children in the paths of right-eousness, justice and holiness.

It is easy to make a shibboleth of the modern nuclear family — to put it on a pedestal and place on it aspirations and expectations that rightly are only achieved by a vibrant faith in God. Parents can often feel that everyone is expecting too much of them — that they be Super-Mums and Super-Dads! However, it is also easy to lose contact with those important spiritual traditions which not only provide a point of cultural continuity but the means of emotional health and well-being.

The call to manage creation and build community is as valid for us today as it was in the time of Noah.

Discussion questions

Talking it through

1 'Genesis 6, verse 5 or Psalm 14, verse 3
present a pessimistic and biased view of
human civilisation — one that needs to be
balanced by the more optimistic and enno-
bling views of Genesis 1, verse 26 onwards
or Psalm 8, verses 5 to 8.' Does human
history support this view?

2 One of the characteristics of God is said to
be his 'immutability' — that is, he is not
fickle and never changes his mind or disposi-
tion. How then should we interpret the
statement, 'I am sorry that I have made
them' (chapter 6, verse 7)?

3 Noah seems to represent a contradiction of
the pessimistic view of humanity mentioned
already — he was a 'righteous man, the one
blameless man of his time, and he walked
with God'.

What does this contradiction show? What

does it tell us about our attitude to ourselves?

4 To what extent is the idea of a loving God and the ethic of loving your enemies undermined by the flood story? How successful was God's reordering strategy?

5 Noah can't have been 'blameless' all of the time, because he got drunk and had serious family problems as a result of his orgy (chapter 9, verses 20 onwards).

Which other biblical figures had family or moral problems? Compare 1 Samuel 8, verses 1 to 3; 1 Samuel 15, verses 10 to 14; 2 Samuel 11, verses 1 to 5, and 14 to 17; and 2 Samuel 13, verses 20 to 22.

Are leaders particularly vulnerable to such problems? Why?

Widening our horizons

1 What light, if any, does modern science —
especially archaeology — shed on the period,
extent, location and effects of the flood?
Look up information on flood stories in the
ancient world. Some suggestions are: Claus
Westermann's *Genesis 1-11: A Commentary*,
J.B. Pritchard's *Ancient Near East: Anthology
of Texts and Pictures*, a Bible dictionary or
Bible encyclopedia.

How is the biblical flood narrative similar
or different? How does looking at this
evidence affect your attitude to the Bible
story? If so, how?

2 How has an optimistic view of human nature affected:
(a) child education
(b) our assessment of politicians
(c) marriage counselling
(d) social welfare?

Is this view right? Are we in danger of
overreacting and becoming overly pessimistic?

3 'Whoever sheds the blood of a human, by a human shall that person's blood be shed' (chapter 9, verse 6). What are the advantages and disadvantages of capital punishment? Why does the book of Genesis advocate it?

Is such a practice compatible with a compassionate, humane society today?

4 'The rainbow seems to have lost its theological significance, judging by the history of natural disasters since the flood.' Do you agree?

5
Spread and corruption of the new world order

Why did God frustrate human pride?
GENESIS CHAPTER 10, VERSE 1 TO
CHAPTER 11, VERSE 32

THESE TWO CHAPTERS OF GENESIS link the early period of human history with all that follows in the Bible — Abraham and the remainder of the Old Testament, where God works with a chosen people, and the New Testament, where out of these chosen people he sends the Saviour of the world. They link our primeval history with the period of recorded history, thus marking an important transition from mythological to historical.

The precision and detail of the chronologies in these chapters, garnered from a very ancient source, suggest we are dealing with real people set against a rich cultural tradition.

The table of nations
(chapter 10, verses 1 to 32)

This list gives no primary treatment to any nation, not even Israel. In this it is somewhat out of character with much of the rest of the Old Testament.

For a nation like Israel that saw its place at the centre of history, such a table of nations represents a contradiction. The story of salvation is premised on the abhorrence of foreigners — Egyptians, Philistines, Canaanites and others — and the rejection of their evil customs.

How then did the table, with its affirmation of such groups, get past the editor? More astounding is the omission of any reference to Israel — apart from the name 'Arpachshad' (verse 22) whose line in chapter 11, verses 12 to 26 leads us to Abraham. Israel's international obscurity is set in stark contrast to her election in Deuteronomy 7, verse 7.

Gerhard von Rad points out that in the period on view, 'two great kingdoms especially determined the history of the Near East: Egypt in the south and the Hittites in the north.' By the time of the table of nations, the Hittite kingdom has disappeared.

A Semitic-Aramean incursion into Palestine and Syria occurred between 1500 and 1200 BC. Gerhard von Rad says that Israelites entered the land as part of this transmigration of peoples.[1] Genesis 10 is recognised as a late composition — probably not earlier than the eighth century BC. B. Oded asserts that the table divides human society into 'three types of communities, each with a distinct lifestyle, each operating in a different setting'.[2]

❑ *Japheth (verses 2 to 5)*
While Japheth is the name of an actual person, the other names in verses 2 to 6 refer to nations or groups of people. Most of Japheth's sons represent, Oded says, 'the maritime nations. . . those who dwell on islands and along the seashores. . . the seafarers, the island and seashore dwellers'.[3]

Westermann says Gomer is linked with Gog in Ezekiel 38, verse 6 and is situated on the north coast of the Black Sea, between the Don and Danube Rivers.[4] Magog is also mentioned in Ezekiel 38, verse 2 in connection with Meshech and Tubal. The name 'Madai' refers to the Medes who were absorbed into the Persian empire. Javan refers to the Ionian Greeks on the Asia Minor coast. Tubal, located in Cilicia, and Meshech in Phrygia are listed together elsewhere in Ezekiel 32, verse 26 and Ezekiel 39, verse 1.

People from Tiras may have been islanders in the Aegean Sea. Oded says that the descendants of Japheth comprised various ethnic groups settled in

Anatolia.[5]   Ashkenaz in Jeremiah 51, verse 27 is linked in a call to war against Babylon, with the kingdoms of Ararat and Minni.   According to Westermann, the Ashkenazi were an Indo-European people who moved from southern Europe, settled around Lake Urmia and were linked to the Scythians.

Josephus the Jewish historian equated Riphath with people who lived between the Black Sea and Bithynia.   Togarmah is mentioned with Javan, Tubal and Meshech in Ezekiel 27, verse 13 onwards and Westermann believes it is probably a city on the border of Tubal.   Elishah is generally identified with Alashia in the Egyptian *Amarna Letters*; von Rad says it is equivalent to Cyprus.[7] Tarshish refers to Tartessos, the Phoenician colony in Spain.   In the Old Testament, the name often refers to a far-distant place.   Kittim and Rhodanim are, Westermann says, the two large islands of Cyprus and Rhodes.[8]   Kittim is a city on Cyprus, but has come to refer to the land mass as a whole.[9]

There is a reversal of order in the genealogical lists, with Japheth's lineage dealt with first (in verses 2 to 5), then Ham's (in verses 6 to 20) and Shem's last of all (in verses 21 to 31).

At the end of the last two lists, the author asserts the division of peoples along three distinct lines: ethnopolitical, by the use of the words 'nations and families'; linguistic, by the use of 'tongues'; and geographic, by the use of 'countries'.

With Ham (in verse 20) and Shem (in verse 31), there is a closing sentence: 'These are the descendants of Ham/Shem, by their families, their languages, their lands, and their nations.' But with Japheth (in verse 5) we are told: 'From these the coastland peoples spread. These are descendants of Japheth in their lands, with their own languages, by their families, in their nations.'

Oded goes somewhat too far when he argues that the author's intention is to equate Shem with the nomadic movement, Ham with the settled or subsistence farming economy, and Japheth with maritime peoples.[10]

In these summaries, Westermann argues we have one of the first attempts to describe the basic elements of the concept of 'people': the land represents a people's living space and source of food; the language creates meaning for the community; and the families or clans give continuity and socio-psychological well-being.[11]

These people then, from Israel's geographical perspective, were located to the far north, mainly from Asia Minor across to Armenia, with some further east and west. As many of these nations are grouped together in the same way in Ezekiel, Westermann concludes that 'the outlook must be that of the sixth century [BC]'.[12]

❏ *Ham (verses 6 to 20)*

The four 'sons' of Ham refer to the south-west Arabian region comprising Cush, which is the region of Nubia in Ethiopia, Put or Libya, and Canaan. Jeremiah 13, verse 23 asks whether an Ethiopian can change his black skin. Egypt is equated with the 'tents of Ham' (Psalm 78, verse 51) and the 'land of Ham' (Psalm 105, verse 23). Put is often described in warlike terms in the Old Testament.[13] Canaan, von Rad states, was still under Egyptian control at the time of Israelite settlement.

The five sons of Cush and two sons of Raamah (in verse 7) are listed to increase our knowledge of the peoples of Arabia. Oded points out that terms unique to the list of Ham are 'city', 'town', 'kingdom' and 'empire'. Ancient cities are listed, such as: Erech, or Uruk on the Euphrates; Accad in northern Babylonia; Babel; Nineveh on the left bank of the Tigris, one of the most ancient and influential cities; and Calah south of Nineveh, a royal residence.

Oded says that the term 'kingdom' in verse 10 denotes 'well organised state-societies in contrast to tribal and stateless societies so prominent in the list of Shem'.

Nimrod is the legendary founder of the Assyrian-Babylonian empire. He is presented in verse 9, von Rad says, 'as the first wielder of power on earth, the first ruler of historical significance' and at the same time a proverbial hunter. The reference to 'mighty hunter' — translated by the NJ Bible as 'the first potentate on earth' — contains the notion of violent, tyrannical power. Here is the first glimpse of political might brought to bear on the ancient world by a legendary ruler — the forerunner and archetype of many despots throughout history who seek world dominion.

The phrase, 'mighty hunter *before the Lord*' (verse 7), is probably to be interpreted as a form of the superlative, though literally it could mean either 'with God's approval' or 'in opposition to God'. Westermann shows that one of the earliest functions of the divine kings was to ward off any threat to the community from wild animals — for example, David's protection of his father's sheep from bears and lions; the image of God as shepherd; and the equation of kingship in Israel with shepherding in Jeremiah 23 and Ezekiel 34.

Pathrusim and Caphtorim in verse 14 refer respectively to the inhabitants of upper Egypt and Crete. The Lehabim are Lybians outside Egypt.

Sons of Canaan are referred to in verses 15 to 19. By naming Sidon, a fishing city, as Canaan's eldest son, the writer includes Phoenicia in the promised land. The next four names in verses 16 and 17 are 'pre-Israelite peoples in Canaan', Westermann says.[15]

Heth (verse 15) represents the Hittites, though probably not those linked to the classical Hittite empire, which ended in about 1200 BC under the might of the Aegean sea peoples.

Jebusites (verse 16) were occupants of Jerusalem and, according to Ezekiel 16, verses 3 and 45, of Amorite and Hittite extraction. The Amorites are placed in Lebanon in the *Amarna Letters* and in the mountain range of central Palestine in the Old Testament. The Phoenician cities listed in verse 19 can be identified with certainty.

❏ *Shem (verses 21 to 31)*
Oded sees in the phrase 'children of Eber' a reference to all Hebrews, though in this context, to nomads who cross boundaries and wander 'from one place to another'. It could also refer to the Habiru, a 'socio-economic class. . . of foreigners, outsiders and not an ethnic group'.[17]

Elam (verse 22) lay east of Babylon, with Susa as capital, where a non-Semitic people from north of the Persian Gulf lived. Asshur (verse 22) was a great power during the second millennium, and regained a position of international dominance from the ninth century onwards, invading Phoenicia, Palestine, Syria and Egypt, before falling to the Medes and neo-Babylonians.[18]

So what? Who cares about all these lists of names?
This often ignored chapter has enormous theological significance, because it shows dramatically how after

the flood God's universal mandate — to be fruitful
and multiply as long as earth lasts — was taken up
by Noah's direct descendants across the known stage
of global history. As it is appropriate to trace the
theological roots of salvation history back to their
origins, so too is it necessary to chart the rise of
people groups.

When Jesus commanded the early believers in
Matthew 28, verse 19 to make disciples of 'all nations. . . teaching them to obey everything I have
commanded you', he was simply affirming this same
blessing of God, not just at an individualistic level,
but also on whole nations, language groups and
cultures. For all of us who tend to be ethnocentric,
this table reminds us that all peoples and cultures
have their place in salvation history. Neither the
Jews nor any other ethnic group had a monopoly
on God's grace.

God's plan is for his kingdom to encompass all
nations and, to that end, he chose as his instrument
of restoration and blessing one of the typical people
groups of the ancient Near East. Israel, as it turned
out over time, became exclusivist in its understanding of God's universal purposes for the
salvation of his world. The writer of Isaiah 40 to
55 tried unsuccessfully to re-establish God's universal purpose by calling Israel back to her fundamental
task, as a covenant people and light to the nations.
It was only through Peter's vision in Acts 10 and

Paul's mission to Gentiles that Jewish Christians began to understand the fuller picture.

Those who have little idea of global mission would do well to study Genesis 10, which highlights the role of the nations within God's purposes. Despite the focus through scripture on God's dealings with Israel and the church, the table of nations sets the context for salvation as that of global history and culture.

This is borne out by the contrast between God's standards of righteousness, holiness and justice and those of Israel's neighbours in the Old Testament and of the world in the New Testament. As Paul says to the Epicurean and Stoic philosophers in Acts 17, verses 26 to 28:

> He [God] created from one stock every nation. . . to inhabit the whole earth's surface. He determined their eras in history and the limits of their territory. They were to seek God in the hope that. . . they might find him; though indeed he is not far from each one of us, for in him we live and move, in him we exist.

The good news *for all nations* is that they fit within God's purposes of creation and preservation, within his call to build community and manage his world. The call to righteousness, holiness and justice was never intended for Israel as an end in itself. A theology of creation reminds us that the God who redeems Israel has far wider purposes in mind. It is only through Paul's argumentation in Romans 9 to 11 that those plans become crystal clear.[19]

The Tower of Babel
(chapter 11, verses 1 to 9)

Though absent from among Israel's immediate neighbours, ancient stories exist about the dispersion of peoples and the building of a tower as a conclusion to the flood story. Westermann says that in one Sumerian text, language is confused because of rivalry between the gods Enki and Enlil.[20] In marked contrast to the assertions of the previous chapter about the diversification of languages and cultures, here we have a reference to a single root language and to ethnic cohesion in the primeval period, when major migrations westwards were taking place.

Originally within a sedentary economic framework, clans and tribes didn't have to move outside the bounds of their own territory. As commerce opened up the need for travel, people met different tribal and language groups, thus coming to an awareness for the first time that other cultures and language systems existed. Shinar (verse 2) refers to the whole of Mesopotamia. Here is a glimpse of the transition from nomadic to sedentary life and from primeval to actual history. The 'whole earth' was on a journey, not knowing their exact goal, but looking for a plain in a valley whose water and sustenance promised a good life to its occupants.

Having settled in Shinar, a decision was announced in verse 3 within the population to 'make bricks and burn them' — a dramatic indicator of technological progress from natural stone to baked brick in construction work. The primitive building materials were stones and mortar; the new materials — bricks and bitumen.

The intention was to build a city 'for ourselves' (verse 4) and a tower whose tip reaches the heavens. The motive behind the decision is twofold: to attain recognition among its neighbours as a newly-formed city-state via some eye-catching architecture; but more pragmatically, to unify its own people at a time when loyalties to past memories and traditions that had been left behind might have been transferred to more glamorous or dominant cultural forces in the new world.

The audacity of the scheme suggests a desire to 'storm the heavens' — to outdo even the gods in regard to greatness. A 'tower' (verse 4) refers to the fortifications of a city as well as to a watchtower in a vineyard, perhaps made of wood as in Isaiah 5, verse 2.

The idea contains within it the notion of a structure of imposing size and was therefore applicable to the Babylonian ziggurats, which were said to rival the heavens. There is a clear association in prophetic and apocalyptic literature with the thrust of pagan culture and technology — symbolised by Babylon which was the centre of Mesopotamian civilisation — and the arrogant idolatry which feeds on the illusion of omnipotence and omniscience. Jeremiah 51, verses 52 to 58, Isaiah 47 and Revelation 18 are good examples of this.

'Let us make a name for ourselves' (verse 4) reflects a desire to be revered beyond their lifetime. Ben Sirach, a Jewish writer from the time of Jesus, asserts that 'offspring and the founding of a city perpetuate a man's name.'[21] There is nothing sinister about wanting to be remembered after death. The Semitic world view was based on the hope of life and meaning being carried on through one's progeny.

This idea is present in many parts of the Bible in relation to God. God divided the waters and sent his glorious power in the Exodus event 'to make for himself an everlasting name'.[22] The name draws attention to a person or, in this case, to the founders of the city-state. Because of the clause that follows — 'otherwise we shall be scattered abroad upon the face of the whole earth' — we can infer that making a name is linked to the anxiety about social disintegration.

The fundamental need to dig roots into the soil and relinquish a nomadic existence in favour of a settled economy seems to have its psychological basis in an anxiety about the future. Its spiritual basis is the alienation from God as the centre point of existence which all cultures experience as a result of sin. When cultural security and collective solidarity depend on things made with one's own hands, there is nothing that can lift the shadow of uncertainty or fear concerning the future. Note Jesus' words on this in Matthew 6, verse 19 onwards.

The rational human being looks to culture and technology for control over uncertainty and the future; the person with faith entrusts the whole of life — past, present and future — to God's providence and grace. This is the thrust of Genesis 12, verse 2 ('I will. . . make your name great'), which serves as a corrective to autonomous human efforts at control over life's uncertainties. The building of a tower and a city is not the issue here; rather it is, as Westermann says, 'the danger of presumption, of over-reaching oneself,'[23] a point explained in Isaiah 2, verses 12 to 15.

Verse 5 speaks of God's 'descent' from heaven to inspect the construction site, suggesting that God was seen in this story as remote from or above his creation — unlike the pictures in earlier chapters of a God closely involved. Yet even here the emphasis is on a God who not only calls his creatures to account for the way they manage the resources of creation or build community, but for the underlying motives of such behaviour.

In verses 6 and 7, God recognises the potential for rebellion because of a unified language and ethnic identity, which serve as a launching pad for even greater acts of defiance. Job 42, verse 2 — 'I know that you can do all things, and that no purpose of yours can be thwarted' — has the same construction as here in verse 7, which suggests that members of this community were striving to usurp God's rightful claim to omnipotence.

God's intervention, therefore, is for the protection of human civilisation as in Genesis 3, verses 22 to 25. God's action in confusing their languages suggests that the unity of language presented the greatest threat. Control of communications has always been the key to military dominance.

In chapter 10, we saw how the geographical and linguistic dispersion of people groups was a direct result of divine blessing on humanity after the flood. Here it is portrayed as a punishment upon a single people group who overstepped the boundaries. The reason for such intervention underlines the main function of language, the facilitation of human cooperation. God wishes to ensure that evil will not flourish as a result of such cooperation.

As a result of the dispersion, the project was abandoned (verse 8). If we take up the earlier idea of creation as a dividing or separating of opposites and an ordering of the chaotic forces within creation, then what we have here is a return to confusion and chaos — not, as in Genesis 6 to 9, in the physical, but in the cultural sphere of creation. It is only through the potential reunification of nations and language systems in Christ at Pentecost (in Acts 2) that such divisions are removed.

The Tower of Babel story links the advance of culture and technology with the historical transition from nomadic to sedentary economies. The need for protection led to the building of ziggurats and fortified towns. The temptation was to place undue confidence in and seek glory from such structures. Materials of the earth — bricks and mortar — were being used for idolatrous purposes — to protect people from military attack and from losing their future identity and credibility.

Genesis 10, verse 10 traces the origin of Babylon back to the political and military manoeuvres of Nimrod. Genesis 4, verse 17 describes the founding of a city by Enoch. The major difference between chapter 11 and earlier references to city-building projects is the role of *ambition*. The writer weaves this theme into both the beginning (Genesis 3, verse 3) and the end (Genesis 11, verse 4) of the primeval story. Westermann says that there is an assertion that human beings 'are in. . . danger because of their aspiration to burst their created limits, to acknowledge that they no longer stand before God, but to be like God or to reach to the heavens with their works'.[23]

Humans must remain within the limits set for them by God; if they overstep these limits, they bring chaos upon themselves and others. Hendel sees the theme of 'overstepping of bounds' and the divine setting of limits, as central to an understanding of Genesis 1 to 11.[24]

God's grace is seen in a preventative role here. Lest nothing else should dissuade those untoward ambitions, he intervenes so that the tower cannot reach to the heavens. The distinction between creature and creator will always remain, regardless of technological and cultural processes. The dispersion allows for cultural diversity and pluralism, as opposed to a dehumanising totalitarianism within such a regime as that of Genesis 11, verse 1.

Despite the divisiveness of language and the snare of ethnocentrism, Genesis 11, verses 1 to 9 points ahead to a divine reversal of the confusion of languages, to a day when 'every tongue shall confess' Jesus as Lord, and when human ambition turns away from the worship of cultural products to that of the Lord of all cultures, peoples and languages.

The genealogy of Shem
(chapter 11, verses 10 to 32)

All that needs to be noted here is the deliberate transition from primeval to patriarchal history via the concentration of the line of Shem through to Abraham.

The story of salvation through Abram, later called Abraham, clearly flows out of the story of creation. If one combines the genealogies of Genesis 5 and 11, Noah is alive at the time of Abram, and Shem at the time of Jacob. Westermann said this led the authors of the Samaritan Pentateuch and Greek LXX to lengthen the period between the flood and Abram by 650 and 880 years respectively.[25] There are other minor inconsistencies, too, concerning Shem and Arpachshad, but these have no effect on the writer's purpose.

Nahor (verse 22) occurs in the Mari Texts and is the site of the royal residence. Serug (verse 20) and Terah (verse 26) are also agreed place names in the neighbourhood of Haran in northern Mesopotamia. The cycle of procreation is underlined by the repetition of the statement, 'and had other sons and daughters'. Significantly missing, however, is the reference to the cycle of death that we get in Genesis 5.

We are now approaching the patriarchal narrative, the signal for which is the birth of Terah's three sons, Abram, Nahor and Haran. Haran dies during his father's lifetime. Ur of the Chaldeans, von Rad says, was the 'ancient cultural centre at the mouth of the Euphrates'; but Abram's place of origin (Genesis 12, verse 4) is Haran.[26]

Abram and Nahor took wives for themselves.

Abram's wife is described as barren, which sets the scene for Genesis 15, verse 2. Terah takes Abram, Lot and Sarai — we lose Nahor — and they set out together from Ur for the land of Canaan. We are not told why Terah made such a move and can only infer that it was part of the westward migrations at this time.

Genesis 12, verse 1 suggests that Abram was called by God to make some kind of radical upheaval. Genesis 11, verse 31 makes it clear that Haran was only a temporary abode for Abram, Lot and Sarai. The destination of Canaan was already firmly implanted in their minds during the first stage of the journey with Terah. And so the link is made, through Abram, between God's original purpose for the creation in Adam and his redemptive plan in Jesus Christ.

The reader is forced to ask who Abram is, where he comes from, to whom he belongs and why he is singled out by God as an agent for such grandiose and global plans. The 'gospel' message here lies in the promise of land, national identity and global recognition for all who express loyalty to him, but with the threat of a curse on those outside such bonds of solidarity.

*   *   *

The background to these bridging verses has been clearly laid out in Genesis 1 to 11, via a number of major ideas or themes. D.J.A. Clines suggests three 'recurrent motifs' in these eleven chapters:

* First, there is sin, then a speech by God, then mitigations, then punishment;
* Second, there is spread of sin, then spread of grace; and
* Third, there is creation, then un-creation (with the return of chaos), then re-creation.[27]

By way of synthesis, he then poses two possible themes: first, people always tend to undo God's good creation, despite his willingness to forgive sin; and second, because of his commitment to his world, which induces his righteous judgment, God's grace never fails to rescue humans from the destructive consequences of sin.[28]

In summary, Genesis 1 to 11 raises some fundamental questions about human existence: What makes people human or less human? What is the purpose of their lives? Where does evil come from? Is there any hope for the world? Why do people always turn against God? Why does brother kill brother? Why is human technology used against God?

And the answer? One answer given in Genesis 1 to 11, Scullion says, is 'simply that it has always been so'.[29]

Discussion questions

Talking it through

1 How is the treatment of ancestry in Genesis 10 similar to contemporary family histories? What is the underlying reason for people's fascination with their own history? Do the genealogies in Genesis have the same kind of purpose?

2 What is the key function of the genealogy in Genesis 11? What does this say about God and families?

3 How did God use language in chapter 11, verses 1 to 9, to achieve his purposes?

4 Why does Genesis 1 to 11 end with genealogies — and with Abram childless and 'out in nowhere land'?

Widening our horizons

1 Do you think language differences today are a hindrance or a help? Have they had a positive part to play in the achievement of God's purposes? How?

2 In what ways are cities destructive of human relationships and culture? Jeremiah 29, verse 4 onwards suggests that we live in them as aliens, but that we must work and pray for the welfare of the cities in which God places us.

Does seeking the welfare of a city mean the same as engaging in personal evangelism?

3 Pride and fear seem to be motivating forces in Genesis 11, verse 4. In what other situations are these two forces at work?

Can they ever be positive forces? How can we handle them — in ourselves or in others?

4 Here's a final review question. Have each group member pick out one of the following themes:

(a) God's purpose for creation and humanity
(b) The distinctive qualities of humans
(c) Sexuality and community
(d) Sin and its consequences
(e) God's justice and grace
(f) The emergence/purpose of culture and economic production
(g) Religion, myth and ritual
(h) The place of the Old Testament in Christian thought and life
(i) Jesus Christ as the fulfilment of Genesis 1 to 11.

Appendix

Genesis chapters 1 to 11 in New Testament thought

There is a close link between Genesis chapter 1 to 11 and the New Testament. This is because the early chapters of Genesis are an important part of the framework of New Testament thinking. We shall simply note these references book-by-book:

Matthew
chapter 5, verse 14: 'You are the light of the world' (cf. John 8, verse 1: 'I am the light of the world.')

chapter 5, verse 45: 'Your father in heaven. . . makes his sun rise on the evil and the good, and sends rain on the righteous and on the unrighteous.'

chapter 12, verses 1 to 13: Sabbath healings (cf. Matthew

24, verse 20; Mark 13, verse 19f; and Mark 2, verse 27f)

chapter 19, verse 4ff: '. . .the one who made them at the beginning "made them male and female". . . For this reason a man shall leave his father. . . what God has joined together, let no-one separate;' also Mark 10, verses 1 to 9

chapter 23, verse 35: '. . .the blood of righteous Abel. . .'; also Luke 11, verse 51

chapter 24, verses 37 to 39: 'As [in] the days of Noah. . . so will be the coming of the Son of Man;' also Luke 17, verses 26 to 28

Mark
chapter 13, verse 31: 'Heaven and earth will pass away, but my words will not pass away.'

chapter 16, verse 15: 'Go into all the world and proclaim the good news to the whole creation.'

Luke
chapter 3, verse 23ff: the genealogy of Jesus is traced back to Adam son of God

John
chapter 1, verses 1 to 5: 'In the beginning was the Word. . .'

Acts of the Apostles

chapter 4, verse 24: 'Sovereign Lord, who made the heaven and the earth, the sea, and everything in them.'

chapter 14, verse 15ff: '. . .turn from these worthless things to the living God, who made the heaven and the earth and the sea and all that is in them. In past generations he allowed all the nations to follow their own ways; yet he has not left himself without a witness in doing good — giving you rains from heaven and fruitful seasons, and filling you with food and your hearts with joy.'

chapter 17, verses 24 to 31: 'The God who made the world. . . from one ancestor. . . to inhabit the whole earth and he allotted the times of their existence and the boundaries of the places where they would live, so that they would search for God. . .'

Romans

chapter 1, verses 20 to 25: 'Ever since the creation of the world his eternal power and divine nature . . .have been understood and seen. . . they exchanged the glory of the immortal God for images.'

chapter 5, verses 12 to 21: '. . .sin came into the world through one man, and . . .death spread to all because all have sinned. . . death exercised dominion from Adam to Moses. . . Adam. . . is a type of the one who was to come. . .'

chapter 8, verse 39: '[nothing] in all creation will be able to separate us from the love of God in Jesus Christ our Lord.'

chapter 11, verse 36: 'For from him and through him and to him are all things.'

1 Corinthians
chapter 8, verses 5 and 6: 'Indeed, even though there may be so-called gods in heaven or on earth. . . yet for us there is one God, the Father, from whom are all things, and for whom we exist, and one Lord, Jesus Christ, through whom are all things, and through whom we exist.'

chapter 11, verses 8 to 12: 'Indeed, man was not made from woman, but woman from man. . . man was not created for the sake of woman, but just as woman came from man, so man comes through woman; but all things come from God.'

chapter 15, verse 21: 'For since death came through a human being, the resurrection of the dead has also come from a human being.'

chapter 15, verses 45 to 49: 'Thus it is written, "The first man, Adam, became a living being", the last Adam became a life-giving spirit.'

2 Corinthians
chapter 3, verse 18: 'We are . . .transformed into the

same image from one degree of glory to another; for this comes from the Lord, the Spirit.'

chapter 4, verse 4: '. . .the glory of Christ, who is the image of God.'

chapter 4, verse 6: '. . .the God who said, "Let light shine out of darkness" . . .has shone in our hearts to give the light of the glory of God in the face of Jesus Christ.'

chapter 5, verse 17: 'So if anyone is in Christ there is a new creation: everything old has passed away; see, everything has become new.'

Galatians
chapter 3, verse 28: '. . .there is no longer male and female; . . .for all of you are one in Christ Jesus.'

Ephesians
chapter 1, verse 4: '. . .before the foundation of the world . . .he chose us in Christ.'

chapter 2, verse 10: '. . .we are what he made us, created in Christ Jesus for good works, which God prepared beforehand to be our way of life.'
chapter 3, verse 9: '. . .the plan of the mystery hidden for ages in God who created all things.'

chapter 4, verse 6: '. . .one God and Father of all, who is over all and through all and in all.'

chapter 4, verse 24: '. . .and to clothe yourselves with the new self, created according to the likeness of God in true righteousness and holiness.'

chapter 5, verses 21 to 33: 'Be subject to one another out of reverence for Christ. . . wives be subject to your husbands. . . Husbands love your wives. . . "For this reason a man must leave his father and mother. . ."'

Colossians
chapter 1, verses 15 to 20: 'He is the image of the invisible God, the firstborn of all creation; for in him all things on earth and in heaven were created. . .; through him God was pleased to reconcile all things.'

chapter 1, verse 23: '. . .the faith. . . which has been proclaimed to every creature under heaven.'

chapter 3, verse 10: '. . .and have clothed yourselves with the new self, which is being renewed in knowledge according to the image of its creator.'

1 Timothy
chapter 2, verses 9 to 15: '. . .women should dress themselves modestly and decently. . . Adam was formed first. . . the woman was deceived. . .'

chapter 4, verse 3: '. . .foods, which God created to be received with thanksgiving by those who believe. . . everything created by God is good, and nothing is to be rejected. . .'

Hebrews
chapter 1, verse 2f: '. . . a Son. . . whom he [God] appointed heir of all things, through whom he also created the world. He is the reflection of God's glory and the exact imprint of God's very being, and he sustains the universe and all things by his powerful word.'

chapter 1, verse 10f: 'In the beginning [Lord] you founded the earth, and the heavens are the work of your hands; they will perish, but you remain.'

chapter 2, verses 6 to 8: 'What are human beings. . . you have [subjected] all things under their feet.'

chapter 2, verse 10: 'God, for whom and through whom all things exist.'

chapter 3, verse 18 to chapter 4, verse 11: '. . . enter his [God's] rest. . . a Sabbath rest still remains for the people of God. . .'

chapter 4, verse 13: 'And before him no creature is hidden, but all are naked and laid bare to the eyes of the one to whom we must render an account.'

chapter 6, verse 7f: 'Ground that drinks up the rain falling on it repeatedly, and that produces a crop useful to those for whom it is cultivated, receives a blessing from God. But if it produces thorns and thistles, it is worthless and on the verge of being cursed.'

chapter 7, verse 3: Melchizedek 'resembles the Son of God'

chapter 9, verse 11: '. . .the tent of Christ's priesthood does not belong to this created world.'

chapter 9, verse 26: 'For then he would have had to suffer again and again since the foundation of the world.'

chapter 11, verses 3 to 7: 'By faith we understand. . . the worlds were prepared by the work of God, so that what is seen was made from things that are not visible. By faith Abel offered. . . a more acceptable sacrifice than Cain's. . . By faith Enoch was taken so that he could not experience death. By faith Noah, warned by God about events as yet unseen. . . by this he condemned the world.'

chapter 12, verse 27: '. . .the removal of what is shaken, that is, created things.'

James
chapter 1, verse 17f: '. . .from the Father of lights. . . we would become a kind of first fruits of his creatures.'

1 Peter
chapter 3, verses 20 and 21: '. . . in the days of Noah,

during the building of the ark. . . eight persons were saved through water. And baptism, which this prefigured, now saves you. . . salvation through the resurrection of Jesus Christ.'

2 Peter
chapter 2, verse 5: '. . . even though he saved Noah, a herald of righteousness, with seven others.'

chapter 3, verses 3 to 13: '. . .all things continue as they were from the beginning of creation! They deliberately ignore. . . that. . . heavens existed long ago and an earth was created out of water and by means of water; . . .the world . . .was deluged with water. . . the present heavens and earth have been reserved for fire. . . But the heavens will pass away with a loud noise. . . and the earth and everything that is done on it will be disclosed. . . we wait for new heavens and a new earth, where righteousness is at home.'

1 John
chapter 1, verse 5 to 7: 'God is light and in him there is no darkness.'

chapter 2, verse 13: '. . .you know him who is from the beginning.'

chapter 3, verse 12: 'Cain who was from the evil one and murdered his brother. . . because his own deeds were evil, and his brother's righteous.'

Jude
verse 14f: 'Enoch in the seventh generation from Adam, prophesied. . .'

Revelation
chapter 2, verse 7: '. . . permission to eat from the tree of life.'

chapter 4, verse 11: '. . . worthy, our Lord and God, to receive glory. . . you created all things; and by your will they existed and were created.'

chapter 7, verse 17: '. . .the Lamb. . . will guide them to springs of the water of life.'

chapter 10, verse 6: '. . .swore by him. . . who created heaven. . . and earth. . . and the sea and what is in it.'

chapter 12, verses 9 to 17: 'The great dragon . . .the Devil or Satan, the deceiver of the whole world. . . the dragon. . . went off to make war on the rest of her children.'

chapter 16, verse 12: '. . . the great river Euphrates, and its water was dried up.'

chapter 16, verse 19; chapter 17, verses 5 and 18; chapter 18, verse 2ff: 'God remembered great Babylon. . . Babylon the great, mother of whores and of earth's abominations. . . the great city that rules over the

kings of the earth. . . a dwelling place of demons. . .
merchants. . . have grown rich from the power of
her luxury. . . all their wealth has been laid waste. . .
the sound of harpists and minstrels and of flutists
and trumpeters will be heard in you no more.'

chapter 20, verses 1 to 3: '. . .no more the ancient
serpent. . . bound. . . for a thousand years.'

chapter 21, verses 10 to 21: '. . .the holy city. . . has. . .
a radiance like a very rare jewel. . . jasper. . . gold. . .
lapis lazuli. . . emerald. . .'

chapter 21, verse 23f: '. . . the city has no need of
sun or moon to shine on it, for the glory of God is
its light. . . The nations shall walk by its light.'

chapter 22, verses 1 and 2: '. . . the river of the water
of life. . . flowing. . . through. . . the street of the city.
On either side of the river is the tree of life. . . the
leaves of the tree are for the healing of the nations.'

chapter 22, verse 14: '. . . those who wash their robes
will have the right to the tree of life.'

chapter 22, verse 17: '. . . let everyone who is thirsty
come. . . let anyone who wishes take the water of
life as a gift.'

chapter 22, verse 19: 'God will take away that
person's share in the tree of life and in the holy city.'

Bibliography

Useful commentaries on Genesis

David Atkinson, *The Message of Genesis 1–11*, IVP, 1990
Provides a reliable exposition of the text and relates it to the issues of our day.

Walter Bruegemann, *Genesis*, John Knox, 1980
A detailed exposition that relates the text to the life of the church.

John J. Davis, *Paradise to Prison*, Baker, 1975
A study by a scholar committed to the historical and scientific reliability of the text.

Victor Hamilton, *The Book of Genesis: Chapters 1–17*, Eerdmans, 1990
A solid, thorough and up-to-date evangelical exposition of the text.

Claus Westermann, *Genesis 1–11: A Commentary*, Eerdmans, 1986
Using intrinsic, original research, the author provides insightful, practical applications.

Gordon Wenham, *Genesis 1–15*, Word, 1987
An enlightening, evocative commentary.

Useful investigations of key ideas in Genesis

Francis I. Andersen, 'On Reading Genesis 1–3', *In-ter-change*, 32, pp.11-36, 1983
A look at particular Bible passages that demonstrate how understanding what the words mean and how the story is told need assistance from outside the text in each succeeding age.

Bernhard Anderson, *Creation in the Old Testament*, SPCK, 1984
The essential issues of the biblical theology of creation in relation to philosophical, ecological and humanistic questions.

Klaus Baltzer, *The Covenant Formulary*, Blackwell, 1971
A succinct, clearly written account of the concept, origin and use of the covenant in the Old Testament.

C.B. Caird, *The Language and Imagery of the Bible*, Duckworth, 1980
A learned, illuminating and interesting commentary on the use of language in the Bible.

Matthew Fox, *Original Blessing*, Bear & Co., 1983
A controversial, challenging plea to right the balance, as the author sees it, by placing greater emphasis on the blessing of creation — God's earliest and most fundamental dealings with us, according to the author — rather than fall/redemption thinking.

Alan Hayward, *Creation and Evolution*, Triangle, 1985
Argues that biblical creation makes good scientific sense spread over aeons of time.

John Wenham, *The Goodness of God*, IVP, 1974
An intelligent examination of the issue of the problem of the existence of evil if God is good.

Howard N. Wallace, 'Genesis 2: 1–3 — Creation and Sabbath', *Pacifica*, 1 and 3, October 1988, pp.235-250
The writer argues cogently that by connecting sabbath rest at creation with the human sabbath, the Jewish people are given a means whereby the sovereignty of their God can be proclaimed.

Useful treatments of present-day faith and life issues raised in Genesis

Clayton C. Barbeau, *Joy of Marriage*, Harper and Row, 1976
A picture of what marriage can be when a couple are open to each other.

Gilbert Bilezikian, *Beyond Sex Roles*, Baker, 1978
A carefully researched biblical survey of what the author sees as the God-honouring practice of non-discriminatory church and family life.

Marva J. Dawn, *Keeping the Sabbath Wholly*, Eerdmans, 1989
Attempts to give us the feel of the sabbath as part of the normal rhythm of life.

Tim Cooper, *Green Christianity*, Spire, 1990
A major contemporary treatment of the relationship between Christianity and ecology.

Dolores Curran, *Traits of a Healthy Family*, Harper and Row, 1983
A list of fifteen qualities shared by families that can be called 'healthy'.

Paul Davis, *The Mind of God*, Penguin, 1992
Written by an internationally acclaimed physicist who sees himself not as a Christian but having much in common with them, he shows how very recent science has validated the existence and continuing work of God in creation.

Jacques Ellul, *The Technological Bluff*, Eerdmans, reprint 1990
A well-argued case for balanced progress that provides a sane assessment of the value of technology.

Jacques Ellul, *The Technological System*, Continuum, 1980
Intelligently examines the power of technology to desensitise us to nature.

Kevin Giles, *Created Woman*, Acorn, 1985
A look at the key biblical passages on man-woman relations.

Wesley Grenberg-Michaelson (ed.), *Tending the Garden*, Eerdmans, 1987
Sets out to right the balance by showing that the Bible teaches not only the domination of the earth, but our responsibility to safeguard it.

Jeffrey Lilburne, *A Sense of Place*, Abingdon, 1989
The author argues that responsible care of the earth means not only cleaning up our environment, but cleaning up ourselves.

John Macquarrie, 'Creation and Environment', Expository Times, 83, 1971-1972, pp.4-9
A challenge to the idea that the created environment can be preserved by the use of technology.

Evelyn Peterson, *Who Cares? A Handbook of Christian Counselling*, Paternoster, 1980
A systematic treatment of Christian counselling as it is concerned with human need, Christian faith and psychological knowledge.

Endnotes

Chapter 1

1. P. Hughes and T. Blombery, *Preliminary Report: Church and Faith*, Christian Research Association, 1988
2. Phyllis A. Bird, 'Male and Female He Created Them: Genesis 1: 27b in the context of the Priestly Account of Creation', *Harvard Theological Review*, 74, 1981, p.135, n.13
3. Claus Westermann, *Genesis 1–11: A Commentary*, p.92
4. B.D. Napier, 'On Creation — Faith in the Old Testament: A Survey', *Interpretation*, 16, 1962, p.33, n.12
5. D.J.A. Clines, 'Theme in Genesis 1–11', *Catholic Biblical Quarterly*, 38, 1976, p.506
6. For example, Job 38, verse 17; Job 12, verse 25; Job 18, verse 18; and Psalm 88, verse 12. See also Brevard Childs, 'Myth in Conflict with Old Testament Reality', in 'Myth and Reality in the Old Testament', *Studies in Biblical Theology*, 27, SCM, 1960, p.33
7. Claus Westermann, *ibid*, pp.93ff
8. Robert Luyster, 'Wind and Water: Cosmogonic Symbolism in the Old Testament', *Zeitschrift für die Alttestamentliche*, 93, 1981, p.8
9. Robert Luyster, *ibid*, p.4
10. B.D. Napier, *ibid*, p.41
11. Robert Luyster, *ibid*, p.7

12. Islwyn Blythin, 'A Note on Genesis 1: 2', *Vetus Testamentum Supplement*, 12, 1962, p.121

13. Brevard Childs, *ibid*, p.40f

14. *Ibid*, p.32. For the Canaanite background to Genesis 1 to 3, see Fleming Huidberg, 'The Canaanitic Background of Genesis 1–3', *Vetus Testamentum Supplement*, 10, 1960, pp.285–294

15. Claus Westermann, *ibid*, p.125

16. D.J.A. Clines, *ibid*, p.500

17. *Ibid*, p.39

18. Claus Westermann, *ibid*, p.140 and Gordon Wenham, *Genesis 1–15*, p.24

19. Phyllis Bird, *ibid*, p.147

20. Gerhard von Rad, 'The Theological Problem of the Old Testament Doctrine of Creation', in *The Problem of the Hexateuch and other essays*, Oliver and Boyd, 1966, p.55

21. Gordon Wenham, *ibid*, p.25

22. Gordon Wenham, *ibid*, p.28

23. Gordon Wenham, *ibid*, p.29; Claus Westermann, *ibid*, p.147ff, Gerhard von Rad, *ibid*, p.55, Walter Brueggemann, *Genesis: A Commentary*, p.31; Nicolas Wyatt, 'When Adam delved: the meaning of Genesis 3, verse 23', *Vetus Testamentum*, 38, 1, 1988, p.14; and Phyllis A. Bird, *ibid*, p.142f

24. Phyllis A. Bird, *ibid*, p.138, n.22

25. H.G. Reventlow, *Problems in Old Testament Theology in the 20th Century*, p.144; see also John Macquarrie, 'Creation and Environment', pp.4–9

26. Phyllis Bird, *ibid*, p.153

27. E.H. Carr, *What is History?*, Penguin, 1961, p.86

28. Phyllis A. Bird, *ibid*, p.134

29. Gordon Wenham, *ibid*, p.33

30. W.G. Lambert, 'A New Look at the Babylonian Background of Genesis', *Journal of Theological Studies*, 16, 1965, p.297

31. Gordon Wenham, *ibid*, p.36

32. Claus Westermann, *ibid*, p.111
33. John J. Scullion, 'Genesis 1–11: An Interpretation', *St Mark's Review*, June 1985, p.12
34. Matthew Fox, *Original Blessing*, p.46
35. Matthew Fox, *ibid*, p.142
36. See the *Appendix* for a fuller list of New Testament references to creation

Chapter 2

1. Claus Westermann, *ibid*, p.190f
2. D.J.A. Clines, *ibid*, p.501
3. Gordon Wenham, *ibid*, p.57
4. Gerhard von Rad, *ibid*, p.74
5. Gordon Wenham, *ibid*, p.57
6. Claus Westermann, *ibid*, p.202
7. *Ibid*, p.206
8. *Ibid*. Also see Francis Andersen, 'On Reading Genesis 1 to 3', p.18
9. Gerhard von Rad, *ibid*, p.75
10. Nicolas Wyatt, *ibid*, p.12
11. See Proverbs 33, verse 18; Proverbs 11, verse 30; Revelation 2, verse 7: Revelation 22, verses 1, 2, 14 and 19.
12. See Lester J. Kuyper, 'To Know Good and Evil', *Interpretation*, 1, 1947, p.490f; W. Malcolm Clark, 'A Legal Background to the Yahwist's use of "Good and Evil" in Genesis 2–3', *Journal of Biblical Literature*, 88, 1969, p.266ff; and Herold S. Stern, 'The Knowledge of Good and Evil', *Vetus Testamentum Supplement*, 8, 1958, pp.405–418.
13. W. Malcolm Clark, *ibid*
14. Gordon Wenham, *ibid*, p.63
15. Nicolas Wyatt, *ibid*, p.15
16. Claus Westermann, *ibid*, p.216
17. Exodus 25, verse 7; I Chronicles 29, verse 2; and Exodus 28, verses 9 and 20

18. Walter Brueggemann, *ibid*, p.46
19. Leviticus 18, verse 5; and Nicolas Wyatt, *ibid*, p.119
20. John Macquarrie, *ibid*, p.9
21. Herold S. Stern, *ibid*, p.414; Lester Kuyper, *ibid*, p.490
22. Claus Westermann, *ibid*, p.224
23. Jerome Walsh, 'Genesis 2: 4b to 3: 24: A Synchronic Approach', *Journal of Biblical Literature*, 96, 2, 1977, p.171
24. See Exodus 18, verse 4 and Deuteronomy 33, verse 7 where 'helper' refers to God.
25. See Genesis 29, verse 14; Judges 9, verses 2 and 3; 2 Samuel 5, verse 1; and 2 Samuel 19, verse 3f.
26. Dietrich Bonhoeffer, *Creation and Fall*, Macmillan, 1959, p.70
27. Fleming Huidberg, *ibid*, p.287
28. Brevard Childs, *ibid*, p.47
29. *Ibid*, p.48
30. Claus Westermann, *ibid*, p.250
31. *Ibid*, p.249
32. For further on this, see Proverbs 7 and Ecclesiastes 7, verses 26 to 28.
33. Phyllis A. Bird, *ibid*, p.138

Chapter 3

1. Genesis 4, verses 17 to 22; Genesis 5, verses 3 to 32; Genesis 10, verses 1 to 32; and Genesis 11, verses 10 to 29
2. See Job 38, verses 8 to 11; Psalm 104, verse 9; Proverbs 8, verses 28 to 29; and Acts 17, verse 26.
3. Claus Westermann, *ibid*, pp.10–12 and 18
4. See Genesis 14, verses 19 and 22 and Deuteronomy 32, verse 6, for example.
5. Claus Westermann, *ibid*, p.303
6. *Ibid*, p.304
7. *Ibid*, p.311
8. Gordon Wenham, *ibid*, p.111
9. *Ibid*, p.110

10. Claus Westermann, *ibid*, p.325
11. D.J.A. Clines, *ibid*, p.493
12. Gordon Wenham, *ibid*, pp.130–134
13. Claus Westermann, *ibid*, p.7
14. Gordon Wenham, *ibid*, p.127

Chapter 4

1. Brevard Childs, *ibid*, p.49
2. Ronald S. Hendel, 'Of Demigods and the Deluge: Toward an Interpretation of Genesis 6: 1–4', *Journal of Biblical Literature*, 106/1, 1987, p.23
3. Gordon Wenham, *ibid*, p.139
4. D.J.A. Clines, *ibid*, p.495, note 31
5. Gordon Wenham, *ibid*, p.140
6. Brevard Childs, *ibid*, pp.49–57
7. Claus Westermann, *ibid*, p.378
8. Gerhard von Rad, *ibid*, p.113
9. *Ibid*, p.157, note 43
10. Claus Westermann, *ibid*, p.419
11. For a discussion of discrepancies that make dating difficult within passages such as Genesis 8, verse 13 onwards; Genesis 5, verse 32; Genesis 11, verse 10; Genesis 7, verses 6 and 11; and Genesis 9, verse 28 onwards, see Frederick H. Cryer, 'The Interrelationships of Genesis 5: 32; 11: 10–11 and the Chronology of the Flood (Genesis 6–9)', *Biblica*, 66, 1985, pp.241–261.
12. Claus Westermann, *ibid*, p.437
13. Bernhard Anderson, 'From Analysis to Synthesis: The Interpretation of Genesis 1–11', *Journal of Biblical Literature*, 97, 1978, p.38
14. Gerhard von Rad, *ibid*, p.125
15. Claus Westermann, *ibid*, p.443
16. Gerhard von Rad, *ibid*, p.117
17. *Ibid*, p.128
18. *Ibid*, p.129
19. Claus Westermann, *ibid*, p.468

20. Genesis chapters 12, 15, 17 and 22. See also 2 Samuel 7, Jeremiah 31 and 1 Corinthians 11, verse 25.
21. For further references to this comment, see Genesis 17, verses 7, 13 and 19; Exodus 31, verse 16; Leviticus 24, verse 8; Numbers 18, verse 19; and Numbers 25, verse 13.
22. Claus Westermann, *ibid*, p.477
23. For references to the importance of the vine in this respect, see Genesis 49, verse 11 onwards; 1 Kings 4, verse 25; 2 Kings 18, verse 31; Hosea 2, verse 15; Micah 4, verse 4; Amos 9, verse 13; Psalm 104, verse 15; and Ecclesiasticus 31, verses 25–30
24. Frederick W. Bassett, 'Noah's Nakedness and the Curse of Canaan — A Case of Incest?' *Vetus Testamentum*, 21, 1971, pp.232–237
25. Gerhard von Rad, *ibid*, p.133
26. Claus Westermann, *ibid*, p.493
27. Gerhard von Rad, *ibid*, pp.134–135
28. Claus Westermann, *ibid*, p.504
29. Judges 21, verse 25b and Romans 1, verse 30 are relevant here.

Chapter 5

1. Gerhard von Rad, *ibid*, pp.136 and 183
2. B. Oded, 'The Table of Nations (Genesis 10) — A Socio-cultural Approach', *Zeitschrift für die Alttestamentliche*, 98, 1986, pp.16–17
3. B. Oded, *ibid*, p.29
4. Claus Westermann, *ibid*, p.504
5. B. Oded, *ibid*, p.29
6. Claus Westermann, *ibid*, p.506
7. Gerhard von Rad, *ibid*, p.137
8. Claus Westermann, *ibid*, p.508
9. See Numbers 24, verse 24; Isaiah 23, verse 1 and Jeremiah 2, verse 10.
10. B. Oded, *ibid*, pp. 22, 23 and 29

11. Claus Westermann, *ibid*, p.509
12. Claus Westermann, *ibid*, p.509
13. Gerhard von Rad, *ibid*, p.138
14. B. Oded, *ibid*, p.27
15. Claus Westermann, *ibid*, p.520
16. Claus Westermann, *ibid*, p.523
17. B. Oded, *ibid*, p.20
18. Gerhard von Rad, *ibid*, p.138 onwards
19. See Ephesians 2, verses 12 to 22; Galatians 3, verse 8 onwards; and Romans 1, verse 16 onwards.
20. Claus Westermann, *ibid*, p.538ff
21. Ecclesiasticus 40, verse 19
22. Isaiah 63, verse 12. This idea is also present in Jeremiah 32, verse 20; 2 Samuel 7, verse 23; 2 Samuel 8, verse 13; and Genesis 6, verse 4.
23. Claus Westermann, *ibid*, p.554ff
24. Ronald S. Hendel, *ibid*, p.25
25. Claus Westermann, *ibid*, p.560
26. Gerhard von Rad, *ibid*, p.153
27. D.J.A. Clines, *ibid*, pp.487, 490 and 499
28. *Ibid*, p.502
29. John J. Scullion, *ibid*, p.16